God, Golf, *and* Great Marriages

PASTOR SAL

God, Golf, *and* Great Marriages

8 Lessons from the Bible That Will Improve Your Golf Game and Marriage

God, Golf, and Great Marriages

Note: Unless otherwise stated, all Bible verses referred to in this book are from the NIV translation.

Cover Design: Debbie O'Byrne

Cover Photo: Rhoades Photography

Editor: Cynthia Krejcsi

http://www.tailor-made-books.com

ISBN-10: 1-941142-87-7

ISBN-13: 978-1-941142-87-5

TABLE OF CONTENTS

DEDICATION

This book is dedicated to my family for the love and support that I have always received from them:

Debbie LoPriore - my wife and best friend for forty-plus years

Larissa LoPriore Littler - the most amazing daughter ever

Todd Littler - my all-time favorite golf partner

Rylee Grace Littler - Papa's princess

Gabriel Peter Littler - my endless source of laughter

Gabriel and Yolanda LoPriore - great parents and foundation builders

And first and foremost,

God - who blessed me beyond measure by putting all of them in my life.

FOREWORD

As a long-time golfer still struggling with my short game, I found Sal's book really resonated with me and I think it will for you as well, even if you don't know the difference between a bogie and a double eagle. I enjoyed Sal's book for three reasons. First, it's very witty and readable. I got a kick out of it and you will too. Second, it's practical. It can improve your golf game if you apply the general principles that Sal offers. For instance, I loved the chapter "Don't Multiply Your Mistakes." I know some men who would think a good golf game and great marriage are mutually exclusive, but there are surprising parallels Sal reveals that you can apply to your marriage. I especially appreciated the marriage advice about an appropriate apology. Third, and most important, it's scriptural. Sal draws multiple illustrations from the Bible that help men, in particular, be better golfers, better husbands, and better Christ followers. If you're like me, you'll really enjoy reading *God, Golf, and Great Marriages*.

Bob Russell
Retired Senior Minister, Southeast Christian Church
Average golfer, married 50 years

INTRODUCTION

God has this habit of doing things behind my back, like not letting me know that the events that took place in the first half of my life were actually intended to prepare me for the more important second half. In my early years, He allowed me to develop skills that served me well in the secular world, like teaching, negotiating, mediating, and decision-making. And although that skill set was valuable in attaining many of the things that the world tells us are important, God, in His infinite wisdom, knew that I would need more than just learned expertise in a few areas before I was ready to make the transition from working for me to working for Him. So in my later years, in addition to giving me a major thirst for a relationship with Him, He gave me some heavy doses of what I had been lacking, such as:

- Humility,
- Compassion, and
- Selflessness.

I know these are God given because they are characteristics that did not come naturally to me. (Just ask my wife, Debbie.) So now, using all the gifts that He generously supplied, much of my life revolves around serving God by serving His people, and I am enormously grateful for that opportunity. After all, 1 Peter 4:10 tells us: "Each one should use whatever gift he has received to serve others, faithfully administering God's grace in its various forms," and that is what I intend to do.

The idea to write this book had been floating around in my head for a number of years. Simply stated, it revolves around three things in my life that I aspire to be really good at. As a matter of fact, I really want to be the very best I can be as a:

- Disciple of Jesus,
- Husband, and
- Golfer.

If you want to be a true, productive disciple of Jesus, you have to read the Bible; therefore, that has become a consistent part of my routine. Years ago, I began to notice that there were lessons in Scripture that could also be applied to my golf game and my role as a spouse. The premise did sound somewhat silly at first, even for someone with a decent sense of humor like me. Could I really take what I learned from the Bible and use it to make me a better golfer and husband? For me, the answer was, and still is, yes!

Contrary to the behavior of some Christian couples I have met, the correlation between the Bible and a good marriage should not be that difficult to see, but the Bible and an improved golf game? Well, why not? I am an outspoken proponent of taking the endless number of lessons that we find in the Bible and applying them to our own lives on a practical level on a daily basis. To read the Bible and not use it in a pragmatic manner seems kind of wasteful to me. Our knowledge of God's Word should not only increase our faith but also move us to use that knowledge to improve anything and everything in our lives, including our marriage and our golf game! I have never put any limitations on the power and usefulness of Scripture, and neither should you.

I purposely wrote this book in a way that would allow even non-Christians, non-golfers, and the unmarried to enjoy and glean something from it. I realize that I am writing from a man's perspective (that's because I am a man), but women will see an equal relevance to their own lives.

Incidentally, if you have ever heard me speak, you will notice that I write like I talk. I don't know if that is good or bad. It's just me. At this point, I'm pretty much done with my introduction, so go ahead and get to the book!

Sal LoPriore

LESSON 1

Be Humble

"A man's pride will bring him low,
but the humble in spirit will retain honor."

Proverbs 29:23

The Bible

Someone once posed the question: What do pride and sin have in common? The answer: Right in the middle of both of them is "I."

For much of my life, before I was saved, I was a very proud individual. I was proud of all "I" had accomplished, all the material things that "I" possessed, and all the gifts that "I" used to become successful in life. God was nowhere to be found in my boasting, and He certainly had no part in who "I" was or what "I" had achieved. My pride caused me to sin constantly in many areas of my life.

Unfortunately, my early Christian years saw only minor improvement. In fact, shortly after my conversion I was asked to be an elder in the church I attended. What a disaster! In 1 Timothy 3, the apostle Paul describes the character traits of a church elder. In verse 6, he warns us an elder must also be mature in the faith, "not a novice, lest being puffed up with pride he fall into the same condemnation as the devil." Paul obviously knew me. I was so "puffed up" that I could hardly fit through a doorway.

"Elder Sal" had such a great ring to it. I was a VIP in the church, and "I" would bring my secular wisdom to straighten out the thinking of the other elders. Being the wonderful parent that He is, God touched me with His loving hand (it actually went up the side of my head) and straightened ME out. I thank God that He helped me to overcome my prideful-ness so that I am now perfect! (Hey, don't close the book. I'm joking!) Seriously, if anyone, anywhere, thinks that Christians (especially those in leadership positions) are immune to pride-ful behavior, they are sadly mistaken. As a matter of fact, Christians can be some of the biggest offenders when it comes to pride.

In Luke 9:46, the disciples of the most humble person to ever walk the earth show us the effects of pride as they argue among themselves concerning which one of them is the great-est. I really would have liked to hear that conversation. Even the original Christians were prideful!

God hates pride. That's right, HE HATES IT! Proverbs 6:16 begins a list of the things that God hates; and at the very top of the list, first and foremost, el numero uno, is pride! Examples of the negative consequences of pride permeate Scripture. Satan gets booted out of heaven for his prideful rebellion. Eve gets evicted from the most exclusive piece of real estate ever (location! location! location!) for her prideful attempt to be like God. And poor, innocent Adam also has to leave just because he was trying to be a good husband pleasing his wife. (Sorry, had to sneak that in there.) In 1 Samuel 18:7, as King Saul and David are returning from battle, they hear the crowd singing "Saul has slain his thousands, and David his tens of thousands." The prideful king becomes very angry, saying, "They have ascribed to David tens of thousands, and to me they have ascribed only thousands. Now what more can he have but the kingdom?" (verse 8) So King Saul went from loving David to trying to kill him, all due to his pride.

In direct contrast, there are numerous verses and stories in the Bible that stress the positive results of being humble in spirit. One of my favorite stories is about young Solomon, who is chosen by God to be the new king of Israel. In 1 Kings 3:5, God says to him, "Ask for whatever you want me to give you." Imagine God allowing us to receive from Him anything we desired. Trash bags filled with hundred dollar bills? mansions? private jets? Maybe that's what you or I would ask for, but not Solomon; he asks only for wisdom. The important part here is how he asks for it. Solomon precedes his request with this humbling statement: "Now, Lord my God, you have made your servant king in place of my father David. But I am only a little child and do not know how to carry out my duties." (verse 7) Saying that, Solomon exhibits absolutely zero pride in the fact that God has chosen to elevate him to this new position of honor. Unfortunately, years later, it will be a prideful spirit that allows Solomon to disregard God's will for his life and set up his own destructive path.

In Exodus 3, God tells Moses that he is to lead the Israelites out of Egypt and into the Promised Land. Instead of feeling prideful over God's confidence in him, Moses, being of humble spirit, cannot grasp how he is going to accomplish this enormous task. It may not have crossed his mind that it was his humility that caused God to choose him. The more we humble ourselves before God, the more He is able to use us to accomplish His work.

If you stop and think about what Jesus did, you will discover the greatest example of humility ever demonstrated. He left His perfect heavenly throne to dwell among His creations in a considerably less perfect world. (Talk about moving into a bad neighborhood!) And finally He was spit on, tortured, and crucified so that the very people who did this to Him could have eternal life. Philippians 2:5-8 explains this perfectly:

> "In your relationships with one another, have the same mindset as Christ Jesus:
>
> Who being in very nature God, did not consider equality with God to be something used to his own advantage; rather he made himself nothing by taking the very nature of a servant, being made in human likeness.
>
> And being found in appearance as a man, he humbled himself by being obedient to death—even death on a cross."

Jesus went from king to sacrificial lamb. Would you do that? That's humility! I don't know about you, but I want that. Correction: I need that.

The Golf Game

Israeli statesman Abba Eban said about golf, "Playing the game I have learned the meaning of humility. It has given me an understanding of the futility of the human effort."

The fact that golf can be such a humbling sport is one of the reasons why so many people give it up. One of the reasons why it is humbling is because at first glance it doesn't look very difficult. There is this little white (sometimes yellow, pink, etc.) ball just lying on the ground or an elevated tee, waiting patiently and motionless for you to strike it. What could possibly be so hard about that?

Think about it. Most of the sports that we play in our lives involve some sort of opponent. In baseball, for example, you are batting against a pitcher who is doing his best to stop you from getting on base. To make things worse, he has eight of his friends helping him to accomplish just that. Similarly, the opposition in basketball not only tries to block your shot at the basket but will also, in direct violation of the Eighth Commandment, try to steal the ball from you. In football, an entire defensive team practices all week so that on Sunday they can give the opposing team's offense a day of rest sitting on the bench.

So now we go back to you and the little white ball. Whatever happens to it, wherever it goes, it's your fault. There's no one else to blame; you are totally responsible.

As a young boy, I had no experience with golf. I never played the game myself, nor did I know anyone who played it. Like all of my friends, I considered it to be a pastime of the wealthy as opposed to a legitimate sport. I was completely confident that if I ever decided to play this silly game, my athletic skills in other sports would allow me to master golf very quickly.

Hey, don't tell me I was alone in my faulty thinking! My guess is there are a few men reading this right now who overestimated their athletic prowess and underestimated the physical and emotional challenges that golf presents. I have a friend who was an exceptional baseball and basketball player in college.

However, in his early golf years, his baseball swing at the golf ball resulted in some of the most errant shots I have ever seen, and his divots tore up so much grass that we nicknamed him "The Rototiller." He must have been asking himself the same question that was asked by the 1983 U.S. Open Champion, Larry Nelson: "If I can hit a curve ball, why can't I hit a ball that is standing still on the course?" For a while, he was very discouraged because he thought the transition from "real sports" to golf would be an easy one. Thankfully, he abandoned his prideful thinking as well as his baseball swing, took some lessons, and became a pretty good golfer.

Experienced amateur golfers know that some days you play like you should be on the pro tour while other days you look like it's the first time you ever picked up a golf club. One day you can sink every putt you attempt, and the very next day even a three-foot-diameter hole would not help you. Therefore, if you don't already have it, you had better learn humility quickly. If not, you will become extremely frustrated.

Choosing pride over humility can also cause you to make serious mental errors while playing a round of golf. Many men, for example, take such pride in how far they can drive the ball (Can I get an "amen"?) that they use their driver even when the particular hole would be better played with an easier to hit, less distance club. Or even worse, some guys will spend so much practice time with their driver that they will neglect the other clubs that really improve a score, like the PUTTER!

Hey, I get it. There is a real adrenalin rush when your driver smashes the ball down the middle of the fairway while your playing partners shower you with compliments and you tip your hat to the imaginary gallery. One time I played a match against a fellow who out drove me off the tee on every hole by at least 50 yards. After each drive he would smile from ear to ear and make comments like "I really crushed that one." or "That's what I'm talkin' about." Unfortunately, his smile would quickly fade after his next series of poorly executed shots, and I wound up beating him quite handily on almost every hole. Afterwards, as we sat in the clubhouse having lunch, I listened in amazement as he bragged to everyone within earshot about how long his driving distance was that day. He was so busy boasting about his long-distance tee shots that he forgot to mention that he lost the match! There is a particular blindness that pride carries with it.

One of the most self-centered and often self-destructive practices in golf is the *ego handicap*. The handicap system in sports like golf is designed to level the playing field so that all players can be competitive by giving the less capable players a chance to win when facing better opponents. To my amazement, I have met golfers who routinely lie about their scores in order to make it appear that they are better than they actually are, thus boosting their "ego." Without me getting into a very detailed explanation of how the golf handicap system works, suffice it to say that claiming to be a better golfer than you really are causes you to lose the advantage of the handicap system and will ALWAYS work against you when you are competing against other golfers.

The golfer claiming the ego handicap really cheats himself because he is too proud to put down his real score; he doesn't want others to know how bad he is. I understand that no one likes to admit to terrible scores, but I learned early on to count every golf stroke I make and report honest scores so that I will not lose the advantage that the handicap system gives me in competition.

At the polar opposite of the *ego handicap*, which decreases your chances of winning, is the notorious golf no-no known as *sandbagging*, which drastically increases your chances of winning. *Sandbagging* is reporting scores that are worse than you actually play so as to take unfair advantage of the handicap system. The sandbagger cheats his opponent; he is so proud that he is willing to cheat in order to win. There are many unkind names to describe people who do this. One of them is CHEATER! If you are a golfer and you do this, understand two facts. Number one is that most people who play with you know that you do it. And number two is, at the very least, they do not respect you for it. If you are guilty of this, STOP IT! Don't let the pride you may feel by winning cause you to weaken your character and destroy your reputation.

Pride shows up in some of the most interesting places on the golf course. In his youth, my father had a well-deserved reputation as an outstanding baseball player. He was so good that as a teenager he was playing on semi-pro teams in his native Bronx with considerably older players. In 1942, he was invited by the New York Yankees to try out for the team, but being drafted and serving in World War II helped put an end to his baseball career. A bit of wisdom that he passed on to me at an early age was, in his words, "Always try to play sports with guys better than you because you will learn from them." I always thought that was great advice. That is why I find it odd that some golfers I know consistently choose playing partners who play at the same level that they do. Don't get me wrong. Because I enjoy golf so much, I will play with golfers at any level; but I personally find it most helpful for improving my game to play with golfers better than me. I normally won't even ask them for advice, but I simply watch what they do and absorb as much as I can. So why don't all golfers (especially men) actively seek out better players as partners? I think pride has a lot to do with it. Let me rephrase that. I know pride has a lot to do with it. If this is you, just accept the fact that there are players who are more skilled than you and GET OVER IT! Don't let your pride keep you from improving your game.

Friends that I play golf with get a good laugh at the backpack full of "necessities" that I always bring to the golf course. Sun tan lotion, aspirin, bug spray, band aids, granola bars, and an extra pair of socks is only a partial list of what I think I may need. Over the years I have learned to make sure I also bring a generous amount of humility and leave my pride somewhere where I can't find it.

The Marriage

Pridefulness in one or both partners in a marriage is often the "deathblow" (Remember those Kung Fu movies from the 70s and 80s?) to the relationship on a number of different levels. Pride replaces "**our** needs" with "**my** needs," "**our** joy" with "**my** happiness," and "**God's** plan" with "**my** plan."

As a Pastoral Counselor, I deal with the consequences of pride in marriages more often than I would like to admit. When I am trying to help a couple reconcile an issue in their marriage and both of them are prideful, I know that we are all in for a lot of work.

Using statements that I have heard couples make for years, let's look at some of the most common examples of how pride helps destroy a marriage. Please read carefully and see if you can spot the similarity found in each of these statements. Hint: THE FIRST LETTER!

• **"I'm right!"** One of the questions I usually ask each spouse in a marital conflict is this: "Is it more important for you to be right or to resolve the conflict?" You might be surprised to find how many would rather prove themselves "right" at the expense of letting the conflict continue. As a matter of fact, both spouses often get mad at me because I refuse to take their side. Frankly, I could literally care less who is right and who is wrong. I simply focus on resolving the issue. The need to be "right" has pride's fingerprints all over it and is a huge obstacle to problem solving and communication in any marriage. Don't waste your time and efforts arguing over who's right because in the scheme of things it really doesn't matter. Whatever the issue in your marriage is, put your pride behind you and choose resolution instead. Think of it this way: Who's right? Who cares?

• **"I'm not happy!"** If you don't know this already, I have a news flash for you: you do not want to be happy! You read that correctly. You don't want happiness; you want joy. There is a big difference between the two. Happiness is conditional. It is based on your circumstances, which are constantly changing. I have a good round of golf and I'm happy. The next day I have a bad round and I'm unhappy. One morning my wife makes me a wonderful breakfast, the next day she tells me I'm on my own. And so it goes.

Happiness is self-centered because you measure the importance of all the events in your life by how they affect you personally. Joy, however, comes from our relationship with God and is not subject to outside influences. The apostle Paul tells us that we can be content in any and all situations based on the strength of Christ, not our own.

If you are not happy in your marriage, you need to ask yourself if you are a **selfless** or a **selfish** spouse. Let me give you a great example of that. I was counseling a couple a few years ago because the husband admitted to having an affair and his wife, although badly hurt and worried about their children, wanted them to seek Godly counsel to avoid a divorce. This immediately told me something about each of them. He had committed an act based on "I," and her response was an action based on "we."

If you are "unhappy" in your marriage, try seeking the "joy" that comes with being obedient to God and focusing your attention not on your needs but on the needs of others.

• **"I'm done with this marriage!"** Oh really? You're done? Is everyone else done with it—your spouse, your kids, your family? Is God done with it? Or does it even make a difference to you as long as **you** are done? Statements like this can give good insight into a person's perception of his or her importance in relationships. People who would say this prioritize themselves in the relational equation. Unfortunately, that type of thinking usually continues as people move on to new relationships that are also ultimately doomed to failure. Remember, no matter where you go, you take yourself with you!

One of my least favorite terms in the counseling world is *irreconcilable differences*. According to the dictionary, *irreconcilable differences* are defined as "findings or points of view that are so different from each other that they cannot be made compatible." That is strong wording that gives no hope for change.

I remember reading about a Hollywood couple that divorced after only a few weeks of marriage because of "irreconcilable differences." I've been married for over 40 years and can tell you that you can't even identify all your differences in a few weeks, never mind determine if they are irreconcilable.

Christians should never use that term when discussing their marriage because it completely removes God from the picture. It supports a belief that there are things that God can't do, and we know, or should know, how untrue that is. We should all be so thankful (I certainly am) that God never says to us, "I'm done with this relationship." or "Sorry, but we have irreconcilable differences." He does, however, say the exact opposite: "I will never leave you, nor forsake you." God's grace, mercy, forgiveness, and love for us are abundant and never-ending. We're the ones who decide to walk away from God. If you are "done" with your marriage, that is your choice, not God's. He can reconcile anything if you let Him.

~ PRAYER ~

Father, you tell us in your Word how much you hate a prideful spirit in your children. Help me to overcome any remnants of that spirit that still dwell in me. Help me to follow the example set by your Son in order to live my life in humility. Show me the way to put others first and to boast only about you and your constant provision, grace, and love.

MORE TO LOVE

Philippians 2:3

1 Peter 5:6

Ephesians 4:2

REFLECTION/DISCUSSION

1. Describe some of your own prideful behavior that
    you recognize in any area of your life.

2. What are some of the ways that your pride or the
    pride of others has had a negative effect on you?

3. In our culture, what are the negative and positive consequences of being a very humble person?

4. Explain how 1 Corinthians 1:31, which reads "Let him who boasts, boast in the Lord," can change the way we view pridefulness.

LESSON 2

Forget the Past

"Remember not the former things, nor consider the things of old. Behold I am doing a new thing."

Isaiah 43:18-19

The Bible

Having grown up in New York City, I have fond memories of all the great street games we boys would play, like stickball, slapball, punchball, and kickball. (You may notice here a common denominator of violent behavior.) No matter what game we played, whether slapping, punching, kicking, or hitting with a stick, at any point a player could shout, "Do over!" That meant something just got nullified and had to be done again. Now of course we all abused the "do over," but we never excluded its use in any game. I remember striking out while playing stickball and immediately calling for a "do over," claiming that a bug at least the size of a melon had landed near my eye as I swung. (That's my story and I'm still sticking with it!)

Based on everything I have ever read in Scripture, I see God as a big fan of the "do over," allowing us to shed our past at any time and start over. In John 3:3, Jesus says to a Jewish leader named Nicodemus, "Very truly I tell you, no one can see the kingdom of God unless they are born again." In the next verse, Nicodemus asks, "How can someone be born when they are old? Surely they cannot enter a second time into their mother's womb to be born?" Jesus then goes on to explain in detail how by accepting Him as our savior we will instantly become brand new people. The people we were before our salvation no longer exist. That's correct, born again. The past is gone. We get a "do over!"

During the early spread of Christianity, a nasty character named Saul took it upon himself to imprison or kill as many of these new believers as he could. "As for Saul, he made havoc of the church, entering every house, and dragging off men and women, committing them to prison." (Acts 8:3 NKJV) Obviously enjoying what he did, he decided to leave Jerusalem and track down the Christians who had fled the area in order to escape persecution. On his way to Damascus to do his evil, he was confronted by the resurrected Jesus and was instantly changed. He became the apostle Paul and the most well-known follower of Christ ever. Consequently, it was Paul who later wrote in 2 Corinthians 5:17 these words to the church in Corinth: "Therefore, if anyone is in Christ, he is a new creation; old things have passed away; behold all things have become new." The conversion of Saul to Paul was a remarkable demonstration by God of his willingness to forget our past! It is the very essence of the term "born again."

It would be difficult to fully discuss being "born again," forgetting the past, or calling a "do over" without including the biblical view of forgiveness. In Matthew 18:21-22, Peter asks Jesus, "Lord, how often shall my brother sin against me, and I forgive him? Up to seven times?" Jesus replies, "I do not say to you seven times, but up to seventy times seven." (KJV) Years ago when I first read this I was astonished. Are you kidding me? I need to forgive the same person 490 times? That's outrageous! Why doesn't he stop sinning against me after I've forgiven him 10, 20, or even 50 times?

Like so many people, I had missed the point. All I had to do was read further (verses 23-35), as Jesus tells a most convincing parable about forgiveness. There was a servant whose king had decided to sell him, his wife, and his children for non-payment of his financial debt. After being begged by the servant to have patience, the king, in a Jesus-style display of compassion, forgave the entire debt. That very same servant immediately went out to confront, physically choke, and eventually throw in jail a fellow servant who owed him money. Upon hearing this, the angry king had the obviously ungrateful and unforgiving servant tortured. Jesus concludes the story by saying, "So my heavenly Father will also do to you if each of you, from his heart, does not forgive his brother his trespasses."

If there is anyone in your past or present that you have not forgiven, then this may be a wake-up call for you. As engrossed in this book as I know you are, it would be fine with me if you put it down right now and dealt with your unforgiveness. However you want to do it—phone, text, or e-mail—just get it done. Don't worry. I'll still be here when you return. I'm not kidding. GO!

I like to tell people that their past is where the Devil lives because he can do the most damage there. He loves being around all those harmful emotions generated by your past, like guilt, resentment, anger, rejection, and abandonment, because he makes full use of them in disrupting your present. He tries his hardest to put a negative spin on all thoughts about the past; and, unfortunately, he is really good at what he does.

Always remember that negative thoughts do not come from God. Once again, negative thoughts **do not** come from God! Whenever Satan tries to upset, disrupt, or distract me with an unpleasant thought from my past, I resist him. James 4:7 tells us that by doing so, "He will flee from us." That's a promise we need to stand on.

The next time this ancient enemy creeps into your head, try saying this out loud: "I know this is you, Satan, so in the name of Jesus I rebuke your futile efforts to control my thoughts. Now get out!" You'll be amazed at how well that works. P.S. If you're in a movie theater, you might not want to say it out loud.

The Golf Game

In golf, the closest thing to my childhood "do over" is something called the *mulligan*. The *mulligan* is the practice of re-hitting an errant golf shot with absolutely no penalty. It's as if the bad shot never happened. Now that's a concept! There are many stories floating around about where this practice came from; and they all revolve around, as you may have already guessed, a guy named Mulligan. If that's true, I wonder what his golf game was like for him to be awarded such a dubious honor.

All golfers have either heard of or actually used the mulligan. I have used it so many times myself that I am a little concerned that they might change the name. I can hear it now: "That was a terrible shot. I'm going to take a LoPriore!" Unfortunately, as popular as the mulligan is, it is not legally allowed under the rules of golf and cannot be used in tournament play.

After a bad shot, a bad hole, or even a bad round, too many golfers are unable to put the bad memories aside and start fresh. For example, I used to play with a friend who could never recover from a lousy tee shot. Every shot that followed on that hole would be preceded by some profanity about his first shot. He couldn't get it out of his head. He had totally lost the ability to forget the past and move on, and the rest of the hole would usually be horrible.

If you have ever watched a professional golf tournament, you have probably noticed how well these players can recover from trouble. I have seen some of them hit only one good shot on an entire hole and still achieve a par or even a birdie. You can't do that consistently if you are dwelling on what happened previously. The great Ben Hogan obviously agreed with me when he said, "The most important shot in golf is the next one."

It was not too long ago that I was able to actually practice what I preach. I was playing a difficult par four that I rarely do well on but not for lack of trying. On this day, I was determined to do well. Even a bogey would make me very happy. So I got up to the tee box and proceeded to severely hook my drive to the left, the ball eventually stopping behind some trees. Ouch! I could have mentally thrown in the towel right then, but I didn't. Blocked by the trees, my second shot was a miss hit low line drive that landed in a fairway sand bunker. To add injury to my already miserable performance, my club had hit a buried tree root so hard that it sent shock waves all the way up to my right ear. So far, things were not going exactly as I had planned. Shaken but still determined, I hit the next shot directly into a sand trap to the right of the green. To an outsider, I was, at that point, looking like the worst golfer ever (note to myself to re-read my chapter on humility). On my last chance to redeem myself, I hit a great shot out of the sand trap onto the green and watched it roll about 30 feet, hit the flagstick, and fall in the hole for a par! Three extremely poor shots in a row, followed by a brilliant one!

For me, the best part of that sequence of events was my refusal to let what had previously happened to me affect my positive mindset. Henry Cotton, winner of the 1934 British Open, quipped, "Missing a short putt does not mean you have to hit your next drive out of bounds." If you play the game of golf, you are going to occasionally, or maybe even often, have a horrible shot, hole, or round. That is part of the game. If you make the right mental adjustment of always looking ahead and not behind, your mental approach to the game, and your scores, will improve. If not, there is always bocce. (No offense. I like bocce!)

The Marriage

Unfortunately, far too many marriages are constantly dealing with the negative effects of events or behaviors that happened in the past. I deal with individuals and couples all the time who cannot forget the negative experiences that they have gone through. They can't forgive themselves or others either. Listen, there is nothing wrong with using the past to teach yourself a lesson, change a behavior pattern, or grow emotionally and spiritually. The problem arises when the past hinders or stops you completely from moving forward in a positive manner. A successful marriage requires each individual to deal with his or her own past as an individual and with their past as a couple.

• **Forgive yourself** - I have found that one of the hardest concepts for both Christians and non-Christians to wrap their heads around is the way that God forgives them of their past. No matter how many times they read it in Scripture or hear it in a sermon, some people still do not get it or they consciously refuse to receive it. A client in deep struggle with his past once said to me, "I've done so many bad things in my life, I don't deserve to be forgiven." He was absolutely correct. None of us deserve to have our past mistakes forgiven. That's what **grace** is all about, and grace is what **God** is all about.

I have also run into a significant number of people who know that God forgives their past indiscretions, but they refuse to forgive themselves. If you are guilty of thinking like that, I am here to inform you that you are being prideful. Instead of accepting His unconditional love and grace with gratitude and humility, you are choosing to diminish God's importance in the realm of forgiveness and elevate your own. Someone who takes that into a marriage is going to cause serious problems. The low self-esteem, self-doubt, anger, and other issues that come with carrying the burden of your past and the inability to forgive yourself will sooner or later sabotage your relationship.

When "John" first walked into my office, I was struck by the sadness that covered his entire six-foot-plus frame. His wife had already moved out with their three young children and was filing for divorce. She could no longer tolerate his alcoholism and abusive outbursts of anger. The children were afraid of him, and so was she.

After months of seeking God's wisdom, it was revealed to John that he had blamed himself for his younger brother's accidental death for more than two decades. His destructive behavior patterns were a direct result of the overwhelming guilt he carried and his refusal to forgive himself.

Listen up! God has already forgiven you, and that is the only thing that should matter. He does not require you to forgive yourself, only to accept His forgiveness. He is your father, and you are His child. Let Him love you, and let Him forgive you.

• **Forgive each other** - On the occasions that I do pre-marital counseling with a couple, I always stress the need for a discussion and acceptance of each other's past. I need to be cautious when I take couples down the "path of their past" because the slope, as they say, can be a slippery one.

There are two distinct groups that I purposely look out for. The first group I call the *open bookers*. I mentioned this term in an important conference call once and they thought I said "open buggers." (Thought you might need to know that.) That person or couple thinks that everything, and I mean EVERYTHING, about each of their previous lives needs to be put out there to be discussed. In theory, this sounds like a great start to a marriage based on a foundation of truth. However, where this too often falls apart is when one or both of them are not prepared for what they hear. (It is at this point that Jack Nicholson screams at Tom Cruise from the witness chair, "YOU CAN'T HANDLE THE TRUTH!")

In one of my most memorable pre-marital sessions, "Angela" insisted that her future husband tell her about all his past relationships even though he had no interest in hearing about hers.

What little I knew about her told me that this would not be a good idea, and I told both of them exactly that. She insisted, and her fiancé, although visibly nervous and hesitant, complied with her wishes. Not only did she want to know about his past relationships, she also wanted to know every intimate detail. Even I was taken aback by some of her questions, and that doesn't happen often. Unfortunately, she was so upset at what she heard that she stormed out of my office in tears and the wedding never took place.

Total honesty can indeed be brutal. You need two very strong, compassionate, loving, and humble people if you hope to have any chance that this amount of openness will work well. Always be careful what you ask for. You may get it.

The second group I ingeniously label the *closed bookers*. With these people, all details of their past are off limits and not to be brought up or discussed. I view that as problematic, since it can have a negative effect on the level of trust that is needed in a marriage for it to be successful. It leaves too many unanswered questions and creates an atmosphere of secrecy and speculation that is unhealthy in any relationship. Getting into a marriage where your past is totally guarded and hidden from your spouse is not advisable. (FYI, when the counselor says doing something is "not advisable," it usually means don't do that!) The sensible couples compromise by knowing that they can be totally honest with each other yet using Godly wisdom to avoid sharing things that may have negative side effects. 1 Corinthians 10:23 puts it this way:

> "Everything is permissible, but not everything is beneficial. Everything is permissible, but not everything is constructive."

During your time as a married couple, it is reasonable to expect that you will occasionally experience some serious trials. Maybe it will be problems with finances, children, in-laws (They want to be **in** your business, and there are no **laws** to stop them.), jobs, communication, character flaws, violations of trust, and the list goes on.

Since you are not perfect, mistakes are going to be made. Many of you have already been there, so you know that these mistakes can range from minor to HUGE. If you are not willing to forgive each other, how will your marriage survive? Answer: It won't!

By the way, although my stereotypical Italian upbringing taught me to "forgive but don't forget," I now see the contradiction to Scripture imbedded in that philosophy. Here is the reasoning I used to eventually come to that conclusion. Matthew 6:14-15 says, "For if you forgive men when they sin against you, your heavenly Father will also forgive you. But if you do not forgive men their sins, your Father will not forgive your sins." That means that we are **required** to forgive each other. Got that? Good!

Next, in 1 John 4:7 we read: "Beloved, let us love one another, for love is from God, and whoever loves has been born of God and knows God." All right, so far we know we are instructed to forgive one another and love one another. Are you still with me? Great!

Finally, 1 Corinthians 13:5 admonishes that "love keeps no records of wrongs." "No record" means it's forgotten, eradicated, expunged.

So if any of us claim to be true disciples of Christ, we must forgive, love, and forget. DONE!

"Oh sure," you may be saying. "That's easy for you to say, Mr. Big Shot Counselor. You haven't experienced the hurt that I have." Well, you may be right. Maybe I never felt the pain, rejection, or abuse that you have, but I have firsthand knowledge of someone who did—Jesus. And His first reaction was to demonstrate His great love by completely forgiving those responsible and offering them a "do over." Should your spouse expect any less from you?

~ PRAYER ~

Father, thank you for creating a new spirit in me. Thank you for the ability to shed my old self and be reborn in you. Lead me in the way of forgiveness towards others and myself. Open my eyes to see the beauty of this day and help me capture every negative thought that I might have about the past.

MORE TO LOVE

1 Peter 1:23

Romans 10:9-10

1 Peter 1:3

REFLECTION/DISCUSSION

1. When you think about your past, are most of the thoughts usually positive or negative?

2. What are some of the issues of your past that are affecting your forward movement in the present?

3. Are you currently struggling with your inability to forgive others or yourself for something that happened in your past? What could you do to finally forgive?

4. Describe how an event that happened in the past caused a "disturbance" in your marriage.

LESSON 3

Deal with the Hazards You Can't Avoid

"Consider it pure joy, brothers, when you meet trials of various kinds, for you know the testing of your faith produces steadfastness."

James 1:2-3

The Bible

Wikipedia defines a *hazard* as "a situation that poses a level of threat to life, health, property, or environment." When I first became a Christian, I, like so many others, had this vision of my new life free from troubles, hardships, obstacles, and the like. I imagined that the hazards of life would no longer be an issue with me because my newfound Christianity had put me in this protective bubble fashioned by God himself! Boy was I surprised when the exact opposite happened! In so many ways my life became more difficult because my decision-making was now based on the Word of God instead of the culture that surrounded me. Wanting to do things God's way forced me to abandon my old ways of doing things because I was now representing Him and not myself. Although it may sound like an empty cliché, I was now asking myself what Jesus would do if He were in my shoes, facing my obstacles.

The negative things we face in life are, unfortunately, a natural by-product of living in a not-so-perfect world. The good news is that our avoidance and/or response to what we face can be quite useful in developing our character and, of more importance, the dependence on God that we desperately need to successfully navigate our earthly existence. The more we appropriately respond to and successfully handle the trials that come at us, the less we will fear those that have yet to appear. And believe me, they're on their way.

In 1 Samuel 17, the teenaged shepherd David wants desperately to fight the nine-foot Goliath in order to save Israel from being defeated by the Philistine army. King Saul's attempt to discourage him from doing so, based on his youth and the magnitude of the threat he faces, prompts a confident response from David in verses 34-37:

> "Your servant has been keeping his father's sheep. When a lion or a bear came and carried off a sheep from the flock, I went after it, struck it and rescued the sheep from its mouth. When it turned on me, I seized it by its hair, struck it and killed it. Your servant has killed both the lion and the bear; this uncircumcised Philistine will be like one of them, because he has defiled the armies of the living God. The Lord who delivered me from the paw of the lion and the paw of the bear will deliver me from the hand of this Philistine."

David had experienced God's protection and provision in his life long before he met Goliath, so the giant did not cause him to experience any fear. On the contrary, he faced this trial with confidence and total expectation of another victory. Bear, lion, or giant, it made no difference to him because he already knew how to overcome any obstacle in life through total dependence on God. In your own life, what others may view as arrogant, cocky, or conceited may simply be your knowledge of who you are in Christ.

The first thing I do when confronted with a hazard in my life is pray. The second thing I do is open my Bible and search for the course of action that I need to take. In 2 Timothy 3:16 we read: "All Scripture is God-breathed and is useful for teaching, rebuking, correcting and training in righteousness." I always thought that the key word in that verse was *useful*, which, by its very definition, means it is able to be used for a practical purpose. Although it may look the most attractive when it is new and sitting leather-bound on your coffee table, your Bible is most effective when it is in constant, hard use. I drove past a church not too long ago that had this message out front: "If your Bible is worn out and falling apart, chances are your life is staying together."

There is absolutely no problem that you will face in your life that the Bible does not speak to. Believe me, it's in there. That is why you need to read it, study it, and put it to use. The Bible is an indispensable tool to all who believe its absolute truth because it is our:

• **Manual** - An instruction manual tells you all about the product you have purchased. I recently treated myself to a new flat-screen television (all the better to watch golf on). It came with a manual that detailed how it is supposed to work and what to do if a problem arises. It was written in several different languages to make it more understandable to a wider group of people. And finally, it included a written warranty to be torn out and mailed to the manufacturer.

I don't know about your Bible, but my Bible functions pretty much the same way. If I were to substitute my life for the flat-screen, I would see how the Bible becomes my personal manual. It details the way I should function in my daily life, tells me how to troubleshoot my problems, and comes in a number of translations to assist in my understanding. But most importantly, unlike my television's warranty, which is limited, the Bible tells me that my life is unlimited because it was purchased by Jesus and extends into eternity.

• **Map** - A map, if read correctly, will give you direction. It will show you the best way to get from one place to another. Many people, like me, have replaced their old paper, folding maps with Global Positioning Systems. Personally, I could not be more delighted because I could never, and I mean never, re-fold my maps correctly. It drove me nuts! Anyway, if you know how to use your Bible and your GPS correctly, they can accomplish the same things. Both of them will show you where you are. Both will describe the shortest route possible to get where you want to be. And both will point out hazards you may encounter along the way and how to get around them.

As we travel through life, we will sometimes find ourselves in unfamiliar and uncharted territories, places from which we desperately need to escape. We may not even know how we got there. It is at those times that we especially need the Word of God to guide us to the place where He wants us to be.

• **Motivator** - A *motivator* is a person or thing that encourages you to take action. The Bible has no shortage of verses designed to encourage us. The better you know and understand these verses, the more you are equipped to use them against the hazards you will come across in your life.

A perfect example of a Bible verse that will help you face this world is also one of my personal favorites. It is Joshua 1:9, which declares, "Have I not commanded you? Do not be terrified; do not be discouraged, for the Lord your God will be with you wherever you go." That is a promise from God to you. If that doesn't comfort you and motivate you to avoid hazards, remove obstacles, and endure trials, I don't know what will.

The Golf Game

When I first took up the game of golf, I used to spend a lot of time imagining my perfect golf course. It had acres and acres of lush green grass. That's it—end of description. Why, were you waiting for more? Sorry, but it was MY imaginary course and there were no trees, no water, no out of bounds, no rough, and definitely no sand. Yeah, I know it sounds a little extreme, but don't forget I was a new golfer and I just did not know how to handle myself when confronted with what I considered to be enormous hurdles that I needed to overcome.

When there was any hazard between my golf ball and my desired direction, I would be struck with fear. Every sand trap looked like the Mojave Desert. Every body of water, no matter how diminutive, looked like the Pacific Ocean. When faced with any hazard, I knew that things were not going to work out well for me. As a matter of fact, every time I attempted a shot over the water, I would be so convinced of my impending failure that I would replace my good golf ball with an old, cheap one. That was real confidence, wasn't it? Hey, don't judge me. Are you trying to tell me that you never did that very same thing?

Golf great Sam Sneed said, "Of all the hazards, fear is the worst." My own experiences tell me that he was correct. It sounds silly now, but I remember the early years when I literally hated the sand traps, especially those around the green. I hated them because I feared them. I viewed them as insurmountable obstructions between me and a good round of golf. I remember hitting shots that were headed toward sand and pleading aloud, "Don't go in the sand!"

This all changed when I learned how to successfully hit out of the sand. After taking only one lesson specifically for my sand shots, I realized what I was doing wrong. First, I was not digging in and planting my feet firmly. Second, I was not aligning my body correctly to where my mind wanted to go, so the two were not in sync. Third, I did not have the confidence to take a serious swing at the ball; therefore, I was not following through with my effort.

It immediately struck me that these integral steps to successfully getting out of a sand hazard were very familiar to me. They were familiar because I had, on more than one occasion, preached sermons on the biblical view of dealing with the hazards of everyday life. I could hear myself encouraging the congregation to "stand firmly on the Word, allow your knowledge of Him to dictate your movement and direction, and have the confidence to follow through and keep going."

I now approach my ball in a sand hazard with boldness because I've hit good shots out of the sand on so many occasions. I now expect that I am going to hit nothing but good sand shots. As a matter of fact, I caught myself once yelling at my ball, which was heading for very deep rough beside the green, "Go in the sand!" I've come a long way. P.S. I wonder what my clients would think if they knew that their counselor talked to his golf ball.

Because I have belonged to the same golf club for more than ten years, I can safely (not proudly) say that there is no hazard on the course that I have not been in. As a matter of fact, there is one particular hole where, over the years, I have lost in the water hazard approximately one million golf balls! Well, maybe I'm exaggerating at a million, but it has been a lot! Indeed, I have firsthand, up close, personal, and, yes, even intimate knowledge of all areas of potential trouble on my course. That does not mean that I am able to always avoid getting into trouble; it simply means I know where all the trouble is. Consequently, every time I play on a different golf course I am at a big disadvantage because I do not have the amount of "course knowledge" needed to keep me out of trouble. That leaves me with two possible options:

Option #1: Stay home! Hunker down. Become an isolationist. Do not travel to other courses where unknown dangers lurk around every corner; where unfamiliar fairway angles and speeds can turn good shots into catastrophes for the ignorant and unprepared; where hidden, hungry lakes swallow your golf balls by the dozen; where dastardly greenskeepers place flagsticks in the middle of ski slope greens. Enough! I love playing new courses, so this is not an option for me.

So I choose…

Option #2: Do a little pre-round research on the course. Hit the Internet. What are others saying about the course? Most golfers are more than ready, willing, and able to tell you about a course they have played; and they are especially eager to share the levels of dangers, problems, and hazards they have encountered.

Don't forget the scorecard. It can be used for more than just keeping score. Many scorecards include drawings of each hole that depict distances and hazards. If the rental cart has a GPS system or you have your own, that is always beneficial. Finally, whenever I make a tee time at another course for less than a foursome, I ask if I can play with a member. Nothing trumps firsthand, hole-by-hole course knowledge from your own personal tour guide while you are playing.

Hazards are an important part of any golf course. The person who designed the course put them there purposely to make your round more challenging. Learning how to deal with the hazards you can't avoid will make you a better golfer.

The Marriage

There are so many hazards inherent in the marriage relationship that I may have to save some of them for the next book!

The first and foremost hazard is the difficulty in choosing the right person to spend the rest of your life with. For those of you who think that it is not difficult, remember that I see the fruits of bad spouse choices every day.

If you are a Christian, the Bible says that you should be married to a Christian. That does not mean—let me reiterate: that does not mean—that you will not be confronted with the same problems that non-Christians have to deal with. It simply means that you both have, or at least profess to have, your personal relationship with God in common. Therefore, theoretically, you should both be on the same page when deciding how to handle whatever comes at you. The Bible calls this "same page" relationship "equally yoked." Subsequently, we are sternly warned in 2 Corinthians 6:14-15 against being unequally yoked:

> "Do not be yoked together with unbelievers. For what do righteousness and wickedness have in common? Or what fellowship can light have with darkness? What harmony is there between Christ and Belial? What does a believer have in common with an unbeliever?"

Most of the couples I see in marriage counseling claim to be Christians and, therefore, are equally yoked. I use the term *claim to be* because as previously stated in another chapter, what you *claim to be* is not necessarily what you show yourself to be. But Christian or not, there are some very serious hazards that, if not avoided, can turn into some very serious problems.

I have found that some marital hazards are a lot less obvious than others, causing some potentially dangerous behaviors to slip under the radar. Over the years I have made a note to identify some common "hidden" hazards in marriages. Based on that, the following are circumstances that all couples should be conscious of and avoid:

• **Extended separations** - In 1964 Supreme Court Justice Potter Stewart demonstrated the difficulty of giving an absolute definition of obscenity by saying, "I know it when I see it." I find that I can use his quote for judging how long a couple can be separated before it becomes hurtful to the relationship. How long, you ask, is too long for a couple to be separated? My answer: I know it when I see it.

In my house, it's easy to "see" when Debbie has been gone too long because I "see" the dirty dishes piled in classic pyramid form in the sink. I "see" my underwear drawer completely empty. I "see" the unpaid bills strewn across the dining room table. Do you "see" my point? Seriously, you don't have to look too far to notice when a separation is causing problems in a marriage, but you DO have to look!

"Phil" and "Noreen" had a great marriage for ten years. Then he got the promotion he had wanted since he started with the company. It would mean a huge raise in pay and benefits and would allow them to purchase the new home that their growing family now needed. They also knew that this new position would require him to travel extensively and for weeks at a time, but they both decided that being apart was, in their words, "a small price to pay" for all the financial benefits it would bring. What they didn't foresee was the pressure and resentment she would feel being a single parent for so much of the year and his overwhelming feeling of loneliness on the road, which resulted in excessive alcohol use and almost having an affair with an equally lonely co-worker.

If couples can avoid long separations, they should; but if they can't, they need to proceed with caution and keep their eyes open for signs that tell them that the separation is too long.

• **Long periods of abstinence** - There is the tendency with all couples to put their sexual intimacy on the back burner when faced with the numerous demands and distractions that life throws their way. I have never known long periods of abstinence to be healthy for a marriage; but if for some reason you both agree to a short time of abstinence, it should not be harmful. In 1 Corinthians 7:5 the apostle Paul advises us: "Do not deprive each other except by mutual consent and for a time, so that you might devote yourselves to prayer. Then come together again so that Satan will not tempt you because of your lack of self-control."

Individuals and couples have shared with me some very interesting reasons why they were abstaining from sex for long periods. Here are a few of my favorites:

"I feel too fat."

"Our dogs sleep in our bed, and it disturbs them."

"The bed squeaks."

"We don't want to miss our TV shows."

"My mother-in-law is in the room next to us."

"It gives me a headache." (I did not make this one up!)

If excuses like these are driving your abstinence, you should seriously consider speaking to a good Bible-based marriage counselor.

If we look at sexual intimacy from a strictly biological point of view, it has some remarkable benefits. It has been shown to

Ease stress,

Improve sleep,

Help the immune system function,

Relieve pain (great comeback for any headache excuses), and

Lower blood pressure.

Couples who regularly share sexual intimacy also reap some positive emotional side effects, such as higher self-esteem, more energy, and enhanced feelings of closeness with their spouse.

You have to admit, these are some substantial health benefits for something that is also designed by God to be pleasurable. God gave us the desire for sexual intimacy for good reasons. Therefore, couples should be very hesitant to remove it from the marriage.

- **Boys/girls night out** - More than a few couples I have spoken to occasionally participate in a night out without their spouses. They are usually accompanied by friends who also go out without their spouses. Many of them consider it a rather benign activity and don't see the harm in couples having separate "alone time" with friends. At the risk of sounding like a fuddy-duddy, spoilsport, wet blanket, old fogey, stuffed shirt, or stick-in-the-mud, I have to say I am generally not a big fan of a married individual having regular nights out without his or her spouse. Believe me, I didn't just pull my opinion on this matter out of thin air. I have counseled with a scary number of couples who had calamitous results stemming from this seemingly innocent practice, so you must excuse me.

However, that being said (I know because I just said it), I am willing to compromise my position on this subject based on the answers to four very important questions:

Question #1: Where are you going?

There are plenty of places that Christians and their friends can go without their spouses. Sporting events, concerts, shopping, playing cards or group games are just a few examples.

If the place where you are going caters to, or attracts, single people who are looking to "hook up," it is not for you. And don't give me that "I can handle it" foolishness. I have heard it before, and I don't buy into it. If you walk into the lion's den, there is a good chance, unless your name is Daniel, that you will be eaten by a lion. If you never walk into a lion's den, there is no chance that you will be eaten by a lion.

Question #2: Why are you going?

"Tonya" told me that she went out once a week with her friends because she needed to take a break from her "boring husband and crazy kids." She told me it reminded her of her "carefree single years," but no one should worry because one night a week was "all she needed." Based on what she told me, I agreed that she certainly did need to get away once a week—but it should be at my counseling office with her husband.

Question #3: Who are you going with?

I don't mean their names. I mean their character, marital status, and behavior. Remember that 1 Corinthians 15:33 forewarns us, "Do not be deceived: Bad company corrupts good morals." If you are married and you are going out with a group of singles, that may be a no-no. If you are married and you are going out with a group that includes members of the opposite sex, that is a **definite** no-no.

Instead of going home to his wife and two small children after a hard week of work, church member "Jason" would meet his single, non-Christian buddies at a local sports bar to, in his words, "let off some steam." Unfortunately, his steam letting with his buddies included heavy drinking, getting into fistfights, and sleeping in his car on a number of occasions. "Jason" would be well served to heed the words found in 1 Corinthians 13:11, which reads: "When I was a child, I talked like a child, I thought like a child, I reasoned like a child. When I became a man, I put the ways of childhood behind me." If the friends you socialize with have a negative effect on your behavior, find new friends. Clear enough?

Question #4: Do they serve alcohol where you are going?

I am not talking about a restaurant or a sporting venue that also serves alcohol. I am talking about a place where the primary source of income is the sale of alcohol. Everyone knows (but some won't admit) that alcohol and wise decision-making do not mix well. Did overindulging in spring water or soft drinks ever cause you to wake up in the morning with a pounding headache and wonder "What was I thinking?" or "Oh no, what did I do?" I thought not. You also know as well as I do that alcohol lowers your defenses and may cause you to say something that you would not have said otherwise. It's up to you whether or not and how much alcohol you drink, but I would be remiss if I did not warn you to be very, very cautious.

• **No budget** - This one is a pet peeve of mine and is going to be addressed in a "short but sweet" manner. I don't know why so many couples think they can do without a budget. "Ron" and "Kate" were telling me about all the problems in their marriage caused by lack of money. Although they both had jobs, neither one of them understood why every month there was not enough money to pay their bills.

When I asked if they had a budget, their response was something I had heard on a number of similar occasions: "We don't make enough money to have a budget." I don't know who invented excuses like this, but if I ever meet whoever it is, I will give him or her a piece of my mind.

Is it any coincidence that I always hear responses such as this from people who are having financial troubles? If you do without a budget long enough, it will eventually cause you financial problems.

Listen to me. ALL COUPLES NEED A BUDGET! Please don't make me repeat that.

~ PRAYER ~

Father, I know that many of the hazards that we all face in life are unavoidable. I also know that with your wisdom guiding me, I can avoid many hazards. I pray that I can continue to learn how to handle them in a way that is pleasing to you. I am thankful for your constant help in avoiding, navigating around, and going through any and all hazards. And always allow me to be a witness to others concerning my dependence on you.

MORE TO LOVE

Proverbs 12:26

Proverbs 17:16

Isaiah 40:8

REFLECTION/DISCUSSION

1. What are some of the relational hazards that you have fallen into as a married person that you did not experience when you were single?

2. What makes you feel that you are capable or incapable of handling the hazards that you confront in life?

3. Have you or your spouse either ignored or not been aware of a marital hazard that became a problem and later had to be addressed? Explain.

4. Describe how your use of the Bible helped you avoid or deal with a hazard in your life.

LESSON 4

Don't Multiply Your Mistakes

*"There is a way that seems right to a man,
but in the end it leads to death."*

Proverbs 14:12

The Bible

Most people who have actually read the Bible would agree that King David's affair with Bathsheba was a colossal mistake. Indeed, it was a mistake of enormous proportions (second only to me not buying shares of Apple in 1997!). But what strikes me the most about that story is the way David multiplied a relatively small mistake into a series of progressively worse ones that brought on devastating consequences.

It reminds me of the cartoon I used to watch as a child, depicting a little snowball that would start rolling down the mountain getting bigger and bigger. As it picked up speed, it enveloped trees, cars, people, and houses until it finally crashed at the bottom, totally destroying the entire town it hit. Little did I know that one day I would use one of my favorite cartoon skits to describe the effects of multiplying mistakes. God's planning and timing never cease to amaze me.

Let's get back to King David. In the Bible, 2 Samuel 11 opens with this verse: "It happened in the spring of the year, at the time when kings go out to battle, that David sent Joab and his servants with him, and all Israel; and they destroyed the people of Ammon and besieged Rabbah. But David remained at Jerusalem." The first mistake that David made, that little snowball on the top of the mountain, was allowing himself to be in the wrong place. The other kings were at war and he was not.

What happens next becomes a premier example of multiplying your mistakes. Not being at war (where he was supposed to be), David found himself on his roof looking at a beautiful woman named Bathsheba, who was bathing.

Mistake #2: He made note of her beauty and did not turn away as a Godly man should. The snowball was moving down the mountain!

Mistake #3: His lust made him inquire about her, showing that he had become interested in more than just looking. Snowball growing!

Mistake #4: He found out she was married to one of his loyal soldiers, yet he still brought her to the palace to have sex with her. She became pregnant. The snowball was really picking up speed and becoming huge!

Mistake #5: He used lies and deception in an attempt to cover up his sin. The snowball had turned into a runaway freight train!

Mistake #6: King David, whom God described as "a man after my own heart," finally had Bathsheba's husband killed and took her as his wife. The snowball eventually became the avalanche that would bring dire repercussions on David and his entire family for years after.

The same questions always run through my mind when I think about this part of David's life. What was he thinking about while all this was taking place? Did he not realize that what he was doing was so wrong? Why wasn't he able to stop himself in the early stages and avoid all the misery that would befall him and his family? Did he think that God was not watching? If we get to ask people questions in heaven, I'm going to seek out David for a round of golf and get some answers while we play. One thing I can say with almost certainty is that David was deceived. Yep, that's right, absolutely, positively, undeniably, Satan-inspired, deceived! The alternative would be to believe that David knew that everything he was doing was wrong but refused to stop, which would be contrary to his character.

When the prophet Nathan used a story about a wealthy man taking the lamb of a poor man in order to expose to David what he had done, the King did not even realize that HE was the villain in the story. David became so angry with this wealthy man who is a portrait of himself that in 2 Samuel 12:5-6 he told Nathan, "As surely as the Lord lives, this man must die! He must pay for the lamb four times over, because he did such a thing and had no pity."

Please don't misunderstand me. The fact that you are deceived and don't recognize the mistakes that you are making is certainly no excuse. Like David, at some point in time you will be held accountable. The real lesson here is seeing what can happen when a single mistake is allowed to multiply.

The Golf Game

Renowned sports psychologist and performance coach Dr. Bob Rotella tells golfers to "hit the shot you know you can hit, not the one you think you should." I sometimes play golf with a guy I will call Doug (mainly because that is his name). We were playing in a tournament one day and his drive off the tee landed in a hazard. When we got to his ball, we saw the good news and the bad news. The good news was that he had room to stand and take a swing at the ball and put it back in play without sacrificing a stroke. The bad news was that his ball had sunk down deeply into the mud, making for an almost impossible shot.

I try NEVER to give anybody advice on the golf course (on golf, that is. I give advice on other things anytime, anywhere.), but I really wanted to tell Doug to pick the ball up, drop it on dry land, take the one stroke penalty, and possibly finish the par five hole with a five or a six. In other words, don't multiply the mistake you made with your less-than-accurate tee shot. Now Doug is one of the best-dressed golfers I have ever met: great colors, everything matching, right out of a golf magazine. So in order to influence his decision I said to him, "Hey Doug, no way you are going to hit that ball out of the mud without getting it all over that nice outfit." Did you catch that? I gave him my advice without actually giving him advice, just a statement of fact. (I can be very smooth.)

Sorry to say, my complimentary, subtle, well-disguised suggestion did not work. What happened next was almost too painful to watch. He swung at the ball and mud flew everywhere, but he missed the ball entirely. "C'mon, Doug," I thought. "Pick it up!" No way! He swung at it again, barely made contact, and watched as his ball squirted about ten feet to the right, out of bounds! Now, according to the rules of golf, he was forced to pick it up and drop it back in the mud, but at least it wasn't buried. To make a long story short (That's ridiculous, since this already is a long story!), he finished the hole with a quadruple bogey nine. To his credit, Doug was able to gather himself and stage an extraordinary comeback, but that one hole probably cost him a first-place finish.

Playing in the 2006 U.S. Open, Phil Mickelson stood on the 18th tee with a one-stroke lead. He was not hitting his driver well the entire round, so I was shocked when he chose to hit it again instead of a three wood or any club that would land him in the fairway. I did my best to help by yelling, "Forget that driver, Phil!" but as usual, my voice did not carry well through the television. His subsequent drive bounced off the roof of a hospitality tent and into the spectators. Amazingly, he was left with an opportunity to control the consequences of his mistake and hit the ball back to the safety of the fairway, but he did not take it. Instead, he attempted to reach the green with an extremely difficult shot that hit the tree in front of him and landed only 20 yards away. That made his third shot another tough one that got buried in a sand bunker. He finished the hole with a double bogey and lost the championship to Geoff Ogilvy. Later, when asked about this now-famous series of mistakes, his comment was, "I am such an idiot."

The average round of golf will give even the best of golfers (of which I am not one) plenty of occasions to make mistakes. Whether it's actually striking the ball badly or making a mental error, it is not a matter of if it will happen but when it will happen. Having accepted that fact, the quality of my own golf game took a quantum leap when I began making a conscious effort to not multiply the mistakes I know are inevitable.

Here are some things that will help you to avoid multiplying a mistake on the course:

• **If you're not hitting it well, don't use it!** If on any given day I am having little or no success hitting a particular club, with the obvious exception of my putter, I leave it in the bag for the rest of the day. Most amateur golfers like me are unable to make immediate adjustments on the golf course, so I am much better off working the "kinks" out of the club, and possibly my swing (I heard that giggle!), at the range. I now refuse to torture myself and inflate my score with a club that's not working for me.

As a side note, club manufacturers took full advantage of our tendency to multiply our mistakes when they first introduced the "rescue club." It is designed specifically to hit the ball out of the rough, out of the sand, off of dirt, and out of trees; and it can even save you from an aggressive Florida alligator. (I'm only kidding; a zigzag run is the preferred course of action.) When no other club will do the job, this one will come to the rescue! Hey, I think I may have a future in advertising, or maybe not. Ironically, I know a good number of golfers who always carry a rescue club that has never rescued them from anything. Play the clubs that work best and practice with the others until you are able to hit them well.

• **Know the rules**. Yes, there are a lot of rules of golf; and, contrary to my former opinion, it is important that you know them. It's pretty simple: knowledge of the rules will often help you while the lack of that knowledge will often hurt you. Playing in the 1987 Andy Williams Open at Torrey Pines, Craig Stadler found himself having to hit his ball, which had landed under a tree. He decided that his best chance of recovery would be with his knees on the ground, so he placed a towel on the wet grass to avoid getting his pants wet. Unbeknownst to him, Rule 13-3 states that doing that is considered "building a stance," and he was later assessed a two-stroke penalty. He finished second in the tournament but was disqualified for having signed his errant scorecard.

During my early golf years, I was playing in a member/guest tournament when my ball landed right next to the line of an environmentally sensitive area (ESA). The ball was still in play by inches; but in order to hit my next shot, I would have to stand in the ESA, which you are not allowed to do. So my partner and I (He had as little knowledge of the rules as I did.) decided that I would declare an "unplayable lie" and take a drop along with the one-stroke penalty. After the match was over, we discovered that according to the rules, the situation I had been in allowed for a drop with no penalty; but I had already signed my scorecard, making it too late. A little knowledge would certainly have gone a long way in that situation.

On a lighter note, the 1958 U.S. Open Champion, Tommy Bolt, delivered one of my favorite examples of why you need to know the rules. At the 1959 Memphis Invitational he was fined the then-considerable sum of $250 for "conduct unbecoming a player" due to his "excessive flatulence" while his opponents prepared to putt. When asked about what happened, Bolt's straight-faced reply was that the story had been "blown out of proportion." My first reaction to the story when I heard it was surprise that even back then, depending on where you were, gas could be very expensive.

When you find yourself in trouble on the golf course, an extensive knowledge of the rules will frequently allow you to make choices that minimize or contain your errors.

• **Think!** I can't tell you how many times in my years of golf that I have followed a mistake with the question "What was I thinking?" Sadly, the truth of the matter is that I wasn't thinking. If you have played golf for any length of time, no matter what level you have achieved, you know exactly what I mean. Did you ever notice how deliberately professional golfers approach each swing or putt that they make? Prior to execution, they will consult with their caddies about yardage, club choice, wind direction and velocity, slope of green, and any other pertinent factors before proceeding. In other words, they are thinking!

If you look in the back pants pocket of a pro playing in a tournament, you will even find a notepad with course information to help in decision making. If you check the back pocket of **my** golf pants, you will find the clubhouse lunch menu. That's the reason why they're on television and I'm not. (Well, there may be some other reasons, such as talent!)

A short time back, I was playing a par four hole where I always hit my second shot over a water hazard on or close to the green. This particular time my terrible tee shot went straight up in the air and traveled a measly 125 yards, far short of my usual drive. A THINKING golfer would hit a lay up shot just shy of the water, then hit his third shot close enough to the hole to save par. But not me. I chose a seldom-used club that I would have needed to hit perfectly, and much further than normal, in order to carry the ball over the water. The result of my misguided attempt was all too predictable. So now my ball, along with the murdered mobster Luca Brasi in *The Godfather,* "sleeps with the fishes."

The Marriage

Let's get something straight right away. If you are married, you are going to make mistakes. If you are not married, you are going to make mistakes. Human beings are well-oiled, state-of-the-art, mistake-making machines. No matter how hard you try, you will never achieve a mistake-free marriage; but if you handle your mistakes correctly, you can minimize the negative effects.

"Monica" sat in my office in total disbelief that her husband had decided to leave her and file for divorce. When he had confronted her months ago about "chatting" on the Internet with a guy she knew in high school, she falsely claimed that he was "just a friend." He was, in reality, an old boyfriend that she still had feelings for. It wasn't long before the proverbial "one thing led to another," and the brief affair happened. When her husband found out, she unsuccessfully denied it at first and then went on the offense, blaming him for driving her away with his lack of attention and communication. Sadly, the only "apology" I ever heard her give her husband was this: "I'm sorry this had to happen, but you know we haven't been happy for a long time." Her sad story can be very useful in helping us determine what to do and what not to do when we make a mistake in our marriage.

• **Don't lie.** Proverbs 28:13 tells us, "He who conceals his sins does not prosper, but whoever confesses and renounces them finds mercy." After making a mistake, the first line of defense for some people is an attempt to cover it up. In the entire history of the marriage covenant, this course of action ranks high on the list of things not to do. When you lie to your spouse about a mistake that you have made, it will usually be followed by a series of other lies that turns into one big mess.

Take, for example, this imaginary, fictional, make-believe, mythical, never-happened situation. I come home one day starving and eat the last chocolate chip cookie that was supposed to be Debbie's. When she gets home, the following conversation takes place:

Debbie: "Where is my cookie?"

Me: "No idea, but you look so pretty in that dress." (sly diversionary tactic)

Debbie: "Are those crumbs on your shirt?"

Me: "No, I think it's pollen."

Debbie: "You told me you were indoors all day."

Me: "Oh, you're right."

Debbie: "Are you lying to me because you think I'm stupid?" (Notice the perfectly constructed, no possible good answer question.)

Me: "Yes. I mean no, I... Hey, did I tell you how pretty you look in that dress?"

Proverbs 12:19 (NLT) speaks to us: "Truthful words stand the test of time, but lies are soon exposed." Once you are exposed, your original error will often take a backseat to the fact that your spouse now views you as an untrustworthy liar. If you make a mistake, you can choose to lie to your spouse; but understand that your present and future credibility will be damaged when you inevitably get caught.

• **Don't shift the blame**. I can get pretty annoyed listening to people blame others for their mistakes. It just seems to me that too many people are making a habit out of that practice. Maybe it's hereditary. After all, Adam, the very first man, was also the very first "blame shifter." According to him, he was not at fault for eating the fruit from the forbidden tree. Eve was at fault for giving him the fruit, and God was at fault for making Eve in the first place. In Genesis 3:12, Adam defends himself, telling God, "The woman you put here with me—she gave me some fruit from the tree and I ate it."

I don't have to tell you how much this "it's not my fault" attitude has permeated our society. From the highest levels of government on down, there is a segment of the population that refuses to own up, man up, or suck it up and take full responsibility for their mistakes. Did you notice how my client "Monica" used her husband's shortcomings to justify her adultery? I would have to think that God views her excuse the same way He viewed Adam's.

I have very rarely seen this type of excuse-making work in resolving any marriage issue. When you make a mistake, take full responsibility. Blaming others will probably not work with your spouse, and it definitely will not work with God.

• **Apologize unequivocally**. When you have made a mistake that affects your spouse, the first thing you need to do is offer him or her a true, heartfelt, no-strings-attached apology. If you qualify an apology by going into explanations or excuses, you diminish the sincerity of what you are saying.

Suppose you come to the realization that you have said something to hurt your spouse's feelings and try to correct it by saying, "I'm sorry if your feelings were hurt, but I was having a bad day." Anytime you offer an apology to someone, you need to leave your "but" out of it. (I hope that came out right.) That particular conjunction is the beginning of an attempt to excuse your actions and has no place in any apology. Your "bad day" does not give you the freedom to say what you want to people you love. In addition, the inclusion of "if your feelings were hurt" suggests that you are apologizing for your spouse's emotional response instead of your own actions. Let's face it. The correct apology is very simple. It goes something like this: "I am truly sorry for what I said to you. It was inexcusable." Write that down so you don't forget.

• **Accept the consequences**. The fact that you didn't lie about your mistake, made no excuses, and apologized unequivocally does not eliminate the possibility of consequences for your actions. To think otherwise would be totally unrealistic. Your spouse is biblically obligated to forgive you, but the timing and conditions of that acceptance may not be to your liking.

In "Monica's" case, she was definitely surprised when her husband filed for divorce. Did she think there would be no consequences for her actions? When David finally realized that he was the villain in Nathan's story, he made no attempt to justify his actions or defend himself. His response in 2 Samuel 12:13 was simply, "I have sinned against the Lord." Later, in his eloquent Psalm 51, David not only took full responsibility for his actions but also did not blame God for punishing him justly. In verses 2-4 David prays:

> "Wash me thoroughly from my inequity,
>
> And cleanse me from my sin.
>
> For I acknowledge my transgressions,

And my sin is always before me.

Against You, You only, have I sinned,

And done this evil in Your sight—

That You may be found just when You speak,

And blameless when You judge."

Accepting the consequences of your behavior may be painful, but it is a critical ingredient when seeking forgiveness from your spouse for mistakes you have made.

~ PRAYER ~

Father, I know that in the flesh I am destined to make mistakes. I pray that you allow me to see my mistakes clearly and quickly. Help me to respond to my mistakes in a way that is pleasing to you. Give me discernment to contain and rectify my mistakes and never go down the road of multiplying one mistake into many.

MORE TO LOVE

Isaiah 41:10

Proverbs 14:5

2 Samuel 11:1-27

REFLECTION/DISCUSSION

1. Explain how a single mistake that you made multiplied into more mistakes.

2. Are you and your spouse on "the same page" when it comes to apologizing to each other? Explain.

3. What was a lie that you told or that was told about you that caused very serious consequences?

4. When you have a disagreement or an argument with your spouse, what steps do you both take to avoid it from escalating out of control?

LESSON 5

Control What You Say

*"The tongue has the power of life and death
and those who love it will eat of its fruit."*

Proverbs 18:21

The Bible

Repeat after me: "Sticks and stones can break my bones but words can never harm me." I meant out loud, so say it again. Good. Now say, "That is a total lie, and I will never say it again!"

If you really believe the old adage that mere words cannot hurt, then you have never been on the receiving end of a lie spread about you or suffered the consequences of something that you should not have said. Words can cut like a knife, and very deeply. God knows the incredible destructive power of words. That is why the Bible is filled with verses about being cautious with what escapes our lips. Proverbs 21:23 tells us, "Whoever guards his mouth and his tongue keeps himself out of trouble."

I wish I would have read that earlier in my life because my mouth was always getting me in trouble. The basic problem was that I usually spoke too soon, without carefully thinking about what I was going to say. Sound familiar?

I really wish I had spent more time thinking on one particular day years ago, before offering my congratulations to the obviously pregnant woman in my gym who WAS NOT PREGNANT! I can still see the wounded look on her face and feel the blood draining from mine. Why had I not learned anything from my mother scolding me in my youth: "Sal, your mouth goes into gear before your brain does!" And why is there never, ever a hole to crawl into when you really need one?

James 1:19 encourages us to "be slow to speak and quick to listen," and no one epitomizes the meaning of that verse better than my friend Jim Kinnier. Jim and I served as elders together in the same church where I was eventually ordained and served as one of the pastors. When you have a conversation with Jim, you never lose his eye contact, and you can literally feel the intensity of his listening. When he speaks, you will most likely hear wisdom presented in a slow, thoughtful, and deliberate manner. In fact, I'm sorry, but Jim is so slow, thoughtful, and deliberate in his speech that it forces me to doubt his claim of being born and raised on Long Island, where nobody else talks like that. If he ever runs for political office, I will certainly demand to see his birth certificate!

When Moses was told by God that he had been chosen to lead the Israelites out of their captivity in Egypt, he attempted to dissuade God from using him. One of the arguments he presented concerned his inability to speak well. In Exodus 4:10 Moses said, "Pardon your servant, Lord. I have never been eloquent neither in the past nor since you have spoken to your servant. I am slow of speech and tongue." Little did Moses know that what he thought was a deficiency was actually an asset that I have been looking for much of my life.

I knew a guy in New York who told me that every time he heard me preach, no matter what the subject, I would find a way to slip in a verse from the book of James. Since I have already done that in this chapter, it would be pretty foolish of me to argue about the validity of his observation. What James writes just always seems to hit me right between the eyes, as if he had me in mind. In chapter 3, he has such scary things to say about our tongues that when I first read it I considered taking a vow of silence and finding a monastery to live in. (Fortunately for me, I could not find one that had a golf course.) In verses 5-8 James warns us:

> "Consider what a great forest is set on fire by a small spark. The tongue also is a fire, a world of evil among the parts of the body. It corrupts the whole person, sets the whole course of his life on fire, and is itself set on fire by hell. All kinds of animals, birds, reptiles and creatures of the sea are being tamed and have been tamed by man, but no man can tame the tongue. It is a restless evil, full of deadly poison."

All right, James. It's a little strong, but you've made yourself clear. If we don't control what we say, there may be seriously unpleasant consequences.

The Golf Game

I distinctly remember the first time I ever watched a golf tournament on television and thinking to myself that the game was a little too subdued for me. There didn't seem to be much conversation between the players, the announcer was always describing the action in a whisper, and there were even officials holding up signs that told the spectators to be silent. I was accustomed to the verbal noise that came from the baseball bench "riding" the opposing pitcher, the trash talk between the basketball players, and the cheers and boos from the multitudes of energetic fans of all the sports I grew up with.

What I later came to realize when I actually started to play the game was that there is a lot of conversation that goes on during a round of golf; but because of the nature of a game where you are competing mostly against yourself, the important conversations you have are with yourself. This is commonly called *self-talk*.

Psychologists define *self-talk* as the continuous internal conversation with ourselves, which influences how we feel and behave. Much of our self-talk is reasonable and useful; for instance, right now I am saying to myself, "I better take a break from writing this book and get the dishes done before Debbie gets home!" However, much of our self-talk is very often skewed to the negative and can create a false picture of what is going on in our lives.

There is probably no better place to find this negative self-talk than on the golf course. Before we even began to play, a friend of mine said to me, "Wait until you see how horrific my putting is." He was not only telling himself that he is not a good putter but he was also stating, as a fact, that he would continue to putt badly on that day. Sure enough, his self-talk did him in on almost every hole.

In James 3, the brother of Jesus compares what we say to how the relatively small rudder can send the large ship it is attached to in any direction it chooses. Proverbs 23:7 (NKJV) says, "For as he thinks in his heart, so is he." Therefore, if you tell yourself how badly you putt, drive, or chip enough times, your body will be more than happy to adjust in order to prove you correct.

A subject that always comes up when I am talking to Christian golfers revolves around the use of profanity. I have come to the conclusion that the use of profanity, which is regrettably common on the golf course, contributes greatly to negative self-talk. Even if the words do not escape your lips, just thinking them can sour your whole demeanor and disturb the concentration you need to execute good golf shots.

Harry Vardon, author of *Birdies Eternal*, wrote, "For this game you need, above all things, a tranquil state of mind." I have yet to hear an obscenity uttered after an errant golf shot that promoted any kind of tranquility. Besides, what purpose do these words actually serve? Horace G. Hutchinson, often called the first great golf writer, said, "If profanity had an influence on the flight of the ball, the game of golf would be played far better than it is." Isn't that the truth? I have met far too many men who profess to be followers of Christ yet have no problem using the most profane language, including taking the Lord's name in vain, while playing golf. If that is you, I suggest you rethink either the words you use or whom you claim to follow.

One day I was playing as a guest with a guy whose negative self-talk on the golf course was legendary among all the members of his golf club. He was a better golfer than I was, but you would never have known it by the way he spoke. The entire round he complained how horrible a golfer he was, even though I thought he was playing well. On one hole he told me he was contemplating breaking his driver in half, on another hole he threatened to throw his entire bag of clubs into the lake, and he promised more than once that he was never going to play golf again.

At the end of the 18 holes he asked me how I enjoyed playing at his club. I replied, "The course is beautiful and the clubhouse is magnificent, but it would have been better if I had a partner who wasn't such a horrible golfer." He looked me square in the eyes and said, "Why would you say something like that?" I answered, "I didn't say that. You did. As a matter of fact, you said it in great detail for the last four hours. Personally, I think you are a very good golfer, but as your guest it would be impolite to disagree with your assessment of yourself."

To my surprise, he took my criticism quite well and invited me to lunch to discuss it further. Since that time he has lost the majority of his negative self-talk, and I have gained a new friend.

People who know me well will hear me joke about my golf game, saying, "At my age, there are very few things I do as badly as golf that I still do!" And I still do it because my enjoyment of a round of golf is not just about how well I play. It is much more about the other benefits a golf day brings. I am attracted by the exercise, beautiful scenery, companionship of friends, escape from work, and the fun of participating in a sport that I can literally play well into my senior years. Those factors have thankfully become the major ingredients in my golf self-talk. Don't misunderstand me. I would much rather play well than play badly; but regardless of my score, I guarantee that I will be thankful to God for the day of golfing He has given me and be looking forward, with great expectation, to my next tee time.

The Marriage

Couples having disagreements is perfectly normal and often appropriate. However, it becomes a serious problem when simple differences of opinion always turn into heated arguments, complete with raised voices, pointing fingers, hurt feelings, and uncontrolled emotions. I recently counseled a couple that had, after years of practice, mastered the art of turning any and all conversation into a horrible argument because they could not control what they said to each other or how they said it.

The majority of arguments that couples have begins with a rebuke, so that is what I am choosing to focus on here. The dictionary tells us that *to rebuke* is "to express sharp disapproval or criticism of someone because of his or her behavior or actions." You can also substitute words like *reprimand, reproach, scold, admonish,* or *chastise* for *rebuke.*

As a less-than-perfect husband (Excuse me, I heard that snicker!), I accept that there are times, few as they may be, when I need a rebuke from my wife. Rebukes given under certain conditions can be very useful in a marriage because they can open up needed dialogue and force couples to deal with ongoing issues that they may have been avoiding for a long time. However, if not used correctly, a rebuke can cause some very negative reactions and open some unwanted doors. To determine whether or not you should rebuke your spouse's behavior, you should ask yourself these four questions about what you intend to say.

• **Is it true?** The line between perception and truth is often blurry. Just because you **think** or **want** something to be true doesn't mean it is true. Any rebuke or accusation has to begin with the establishment of what is perception and what is truth.

Back in the day (actually WAY back in the day) when I was a freshman in college, my philosophy professor told us that "perception is reality;" and at 19 years old, I took that statement literally and thought it was pretty profound. Today, older and hopefully wiser, I understand more clearly the significance of that statement. Although it is true that a person's perception may be reality to him or her, it does not mean that what the person perceives is necessarily true. I have met with women with serious eating disorders who look at their emaciated bodies in the mirror and see an obese person. That is definitely reality to them, but it is not the truth.

If you continually make perceived but untrue statements each time you rebuke, you will quickly lose credibility with your spouse; and eventually even true statements will not be taken seriously. Making sure that we speak only truth should definitely encourage us all to avoid truth killing words like *never* and *always*.

The example I am about to use is completely fictitious, and any resemblance to real people is a coincidence. If wife "D" accuses husband "S" of "never" doing the dishes, he only has to point out ONE time in over 40 years of marriage that he performed that ghastly duty in order to justify his claim that she "always" exaggerates. Not that he would do that, since he is an exceptional husband. Seriously, if it is not absolutely, factually true, do not say it!

• **Is it you?** I find it interesting that people can so easily spot their own character flaws in others. In Matthew 7:3 Jesus asks, "Why do you look at the speck of sawdust in your brother's eye and pay no attention to the plank in your own eye?" I reason that we recognize everyone else's "specks" because they are first cousins to our own "planks."

I remember years ago coming home from a very long and intense mediation session that did not go well because of one individual who I perceived was letting his pride get in the way of a successful resolution. So there I was, maintaining my client's confidentiality while venting to my wife about how prideful he was, when she stopped me cold and said, "Excuse me, is that a very large plank I see?" Although I was indignant at first, it soon became clear to me, as much as I hated to admit it, that she was correct. This man obviously bothered me so much because over my lifetime I have had my own struggles with pride—and who knew that better than my own wife?

My recent client "Tom" is a self-described "insanely jealous husband" who obsessively accuses his wife of infidelity, even though she has never given him the slightest reason to justify his accusations. Upon questioning, he admitted to me that he suffered from a lustful nature and not a day went by without him "fantasizing" about other women. His accusations had nothing to do with her and everything to do with him. Because he lusted after other women, he unjustly assumed that his wife lusted for other men. Before you rebuke your spouse, take a quick look in the mirror.

• **Is it necessary?** Rebuking a spouse's behavior can be very confrontational; therefore, you need to make sure that it is a necessary step to take. A very effective way to determine if a rebuke is necessary is to ask yourself what you hope to accomplish by stating it. "Getting something off your chest" or "being fed up" with a spouse's behavior is not, by itself, a good reason for a rebuke. It is simply a strong indicator that some behavior is causing a disruption in your marriage and therefore needs to be addressed.

Recognizing your spouse's need to change a behavior is the easy part. The hard part is determining what you are willing to do to help that change take place. If you take on the task of rebuking someone's behavior, it behooves (I love that word) you to present to that person the correct, alternate behavior. In John 4, Jesus not only speaks the truth to the promiscuous Samaritan woman at the well about changing her lifestyle but He also offers her an alternative way to live, which is following Him. In verse 13 He tells her, "Everyone who drinks this water will be thirsty again, but whoever drinks the water I give him will never thirst."

The apostle Paul knew the importance of using a rebuke for positive change. In 2 Timothy 4:2, he writes, "Preach the Word; be prepared in season and out of season; correct, rebuke, and encourage—with great patience and careful instruction." Paul gives us the perfect three-step process: recognize that a behavior needs to be corrected; then purposefully rebuke that behavior; and, finally, patiently instruct and encourage a behavioral change. That sure beats rebuking your spouse to "get something off your chest."

• **Is it loving?** When I am being rebuked by Debbie for anything (Did I already mention how rare that is?), it is important to me that what she says is grounded in her love for me. Since I trust her to have my best interests in her heart, I will receive what she has to say to me. That doesn't mean that I have to agree with what she says. It simply means that I believe she has earned the right to say it. I hope you can see the difference.

Proverbs 27:6 tells us that "wounds from a friend can be trusted, but an enemy multiplies kisses." If you don't have that loving trust in your marriage partner, even legitimate criticisms or "wounds" will not be received.

A guideline I recommend to all the couples I counsel is to make a habit of never rebuking anyone, especially a spouse, when you are unable to do so in a loving fashion. If you are angry or upset, you are better off waiting until you cool down. That practice has a dual benefit of encouraging both positive communication and spiritual growth. As the apostle Paul puts it in Ephesians 4:15, "Instead, speaking the truth in love, we will in all things grow up into him who is the head, that is, Christ."

Now listen carefully because this is REALLY important for you to understand. It is imperative that you do not lose sight of the fact that you are rebuking your spouse's behavior, NOT your spouse! Couples absolutely need to make that distinction.

I'm often frustrated in marriage counseling sessions when one or both partners don't get this concept. After only 15 minutes of the first counseling session, "Jane" pointed to her husband and proclaimed, "I hate him!" I purposely leaned back and quietly posed the question in my most counselor-like tone, "Do you hate him, or do you hate his behavior?" At that, she leaped out of her chair and screamed at the top of her lungs, "You're right. I hate his behavior AND I hate him!"

I think she may have missed my point. If couples are not able to separate their love for their spouse from the behavior of their spouse, it will be extremely difficult to resolve important marital issues.

Remember, God loves us unconditionally; and because of that love, He will often convict and correct our unacceptable behavior. He needs to be our model for rebuking our spouse in love.

~ *PRAYER* ~

Father, your Word describes so vividly the destructive power that the tongue can have. Put a guard over my mouth so that nothing offensive to you can ever escape it. Teach me to be slow to speak and quick to listen. Allow me to bless all those around me with words of truth wrapped in your unconditional love.

MORE TO LOVE

Ephesians 6:19-20

Luke 6:45

Ephesians 4:29

REFLECTION/DISCUSSION

1. What was the last thing you said that you would very much like to take back? Why would you like to take it back?

2. Describe the negative consequences of something that your spouse once said to you.

3. When you have to say anything important to someone, describe what kind of preparation you normally go through before you say it.

4. Think of an example of how your positive or negative "self-talk" has affected your behavior.

LESSON 6

Seek Advice

"Bad advice is a deadly trap,
but good advice is like a shield."

Proverbs 12:6 (CEV)

The Bible

The Bible is filled with bad advice. No wait, that didn't come out right. I meant to say, the Bible is filled with stories **about** bad advice. Whew, good thing I caught that. I almost delivered a world-class talking point for every atheist on the planet!

1 Kings 12 tells the story of Rehoboam, the son of King Solomon who had the opportunity to rule Israel as heir to the throne. The advice he got from the older men (elders) was to "be a servant to these people today, and serve them, and answer them, and speak good words to them, and they will be your servants forever." (verse 7) Serving the people who follow you and being kind to them is the mark of any good leader. We see this clearly in the ministry of Jesus, as well as the management philosophies of successful modern-day CEOs.

It would have made perfect sense for Rehoboam to accept and implement the counsel he received from the elders. "But he rejected the advice which the elders had given him and instead consulted with the young men who had grown up with him." (verse 8) The advice he got from his buddies was to be very harsh with his people and greatly increase their daily burdens. Unfortunately, Rehoboam listened to the advice of his friends and told his people, "My father made your yoke heavy, but I will add to your yoke; my father chastised you with whips, but I will chastise you with scourges." (verse 14) The people were so distraught over the new king's direction that they rebelled against him, thus splitting the kingdom. So much for advice from your friends!

My personal favorite bad advice story is found in 2 Samuel 13. King David's son Amnon approached his advisor Jonadab and told him that he was madly in love with a beautiful girl— not just in love, but as verse 2 recounts, "He was so obsessed with her that he made himself ill." Now that sounds harmless and even romantic, except for the fact that this girl he was in love with was his half sister!

Now if I had been Jonadab, I would have told my friend to go take a cold shower and forget about it. (Actually, the proper NYC Italian pronunciation is "fuhgeddaboudit.") But Jonadab, displaying an extraordinary lack of common sense, formulated a plan to help Amnon, who then proceeded to rape his own sister. Both the short- and long-term consequences of that action were disastrous; and Jonadab, in my humble opinion, goes down in Bible history as the poster boy for giving bad advice.

Thankfully, the Bible also supplies us with wonderful stories about good advice. In Genesis 41, the slave Joseph told Pharaoh that Egypt must store up grain for the upcoming famine that God had revealed to him. Pharaoh heeded this wisdom of Joseph, and Egypt not only survived the famine but also had so much surplus they were able to sell the excess for profit. Verse 49 says, "And Joseph gathered grain as the sand of the sea, very much until he stopped counting, for it could not be measured." Joseph's advice was so good and worked out so well that Pharaoh appointed him second in command of all Egypt.

In chapter 4 of the book named after him, Daniel gave solid advice to the prideful Babylonian king, Nebuchadnezzar. (His friends called him Neb.) The King was given a dream by God and Daniel was summoned to interpret what it meant. He informed the King that the dream was a warning to him to humble himself and recognize that his authority and wealth were from God and not of his own making. The King rejected the advice and was severely punished by God for seven years. However, he eventually repented, and God restored him. In verse 37 the King declared, "Now I, Nebuchadnezzar, praise and extol and honor the King of heaven, all of whose works are truth and His ways just. And those who walk in pride He is able to put down." Had the King taken Daniel's advice when it was given to him, he would have saved himself from some very unpleasant circumstances.

It is no coincidence that the advice given by both Joseph and Daniel was based on what they had heard from God. The best advice is the advice that comes from God because He is the ultimate source of wisdom. Not only is God the ultimate source of wisdom, He also allows us to ask for and receive all the wisdom we need in our lives. We are assured of this in James 1:5: "If any of you lacks wisdom, you should ask God, who gives generously to all without finding fault, and it will be given to him."

We can even pray for wisdom for others. When I first became a Pastoral Counselor, my wife Debbie prayed constantly that God would continue to generously supply me with HIS wisdom so that all my advice to clients would really be coming from Him. I am always in awe of how He answered her prayers and continuously enables me to serve Him and His people.

The Golf Game

When I first started playing golf in my early 30s (I said in MY early 30s, not in THE early '30s!), I was not that good. Why are you smirking? If you must know, I stank. Are you happy now? But because I enjoyed everything about the game, I was really intent on improving as quickly as possible, so I began asking people about going to a golf instructor for some lessons.

I found it so interesting that all my friends who stank like me were opposed to taking lessons based on a mile-long list of reasons. It's too expensive; you'll get better on your own; and you simply need to play more often were just a few. But I figured if that was true, why did they still stink? Probably because if no one points out and helps you correct your bad habits, you can never get better at anything. In direct contrast to my ill-advised friends, all the really good golfers I met emphasized the necessity of golf lessons in order get to where I wanted to be.

So there it was in front of me: the stinky golfers said no lessons and the good golfers (who I am sure were once stinky themselves) said take lessons. I didn't have to be an aeronautical engineer (rocket scientist) to figure out what to do. I had read that golf legend Jack Nicklaus said, "Don't be too proud to take a lesson. I'm not." So I thought if the "Golden Bear" took lessons, so could I, and off I went to find a suitable golf teacher.

Whether you realize it or not, it is important that anyone who teaches you anything should know how to teach. Did you ever notice that most of the coaches in major league sports were not great players themselves? That's because you need one set of skills to be a great player and a totally different set of skills to teach someone else what you know.

My first golf lesson was a great example of how not to teach a beginning golfer. My instructor told me, "Before you swing, think about your grip, your stance, your knees bent, your left shoulder up, your left arm straight, and keep your head down!" Are you kidding? Anything else you want me to think about? Why not add world peace, putting a man on Mars, and the lyrics to "Hey Jude" while you're at it? Comedienne Phyllis Diller once said, "The reason the pro tells you to keep your head down is so you can't see him laughing." Based on my first lesson, I think there may be some truth to her joke.

In my mind, that first experience just magnified in my mind the importance of not only getting the right advice but getting it from the right person. When I finally found the right instructor, my golf game improved dramatically and I was hooked. Presently, whenever I am struggling with a particular part of my game, I immediately seek advice from one of the instructors that I have had previous success with. I absolutely recommend that you do the same.

The Marriage

Whenever I am counseling couples in crisis, I can be pretty much assured that I am not the only one from whom they are getting solicited or unsolicited advice. Anytime people face problems in their lives, "advisors" appear from everywhere. This is unfortunate, since people going through serious relationship problems can be highly vulnerable to outside influences. My mother used to say, "Opinions are like noses, everyone has one and they all smell." Actually, I had to change the wording a little, but you get the picture.

One of the most commonly quoted Scripture verses that is used to justify the seeking of advice is Proverbs 15:22 (ESV), which reads, "Without counsel plans fail, but with many advisors they succeed." Just like everything else in the Bible, there is a lot of wisdom in that verse; but you need to make sure you clearly understand what it means before you attempt to stand on it. The two operative words in that verse are *advisors* and *many*. The dictionary tells us that an *advisor* is "a person who gives advice, typically someone who is an expert in a particular field." That would mean that the word *many* in the Bible verse refers only to those with "expertise."

As is my custom, I asked a couple recently how many people they were asking for marriage advice. The husband came up with 13, and the wife was up to 22 when I cut her off. So this couple, combined, knew a minimum of 35 experts in the field of marriage counseling? I don't think so! Remember, the fact that someone has been married a long time or appears to have a healthy marriage, while admirable, does not necessarily qualify him or her as an expert on marriage or counseling.

I know it may sound self-serving, but if I had a serious marriage issue that my wife and I could not reconcile, I would not hesitate for a moment to find a Christian Counselor. And beware: merely having the title of "Christian Counselor" does not automatically mean that the person possesses the level of Christianity or counseling skills to be truly effective.

Here are three powerful characteristics of an effective Christian Counselor:

1. one who is a mature, loving, and compassionate Christian in both word and deed;
2. one who emphasizes the role of the Father, Son, and Holy Spirit in bringing understanding, healing, and reconciliation to the marriage;
3. one who incorporates God's Word and prayer into each counseling session.

When I first met "Julie," her life was a total mess. Her ex-husband had put her and her three children through some of the worst trauma that I had ever come in contact with. The aftermath of her divorce left her in a severe state of guilt, regret, confusion, and low self-esteem.

The original counseling that she received was not Christian counseling, and God was nowhere to be seen in her sessions. Unlike secular counselors, I knew that it would take an intercession by God and a woman with extraordinary perseverance to bring true healing to her and her children. Three years of counseling, which included countless boxes of tissues, endless prayer, my insistence on her answering my questions, and her very hard work, has brought her to a place in her life that is light years from where she was.

It was through His grace and His wisdom that she was able to turn her life around. I was just a willing vessel that God used to help her see the direction that would lead her to His plan for her life. "Julie" now revels in the true joy that only God can bring as she raises her children in a Christian home and waits patiently for the future husband that she knows will be, in her words, "God's best."

So now that I have told you where you should go to seek advice, let me point out where you should not go. The following are some of the most commonly used but least effective, and often counter-productive, sources of advice for marriage problems:

• **People too close to you** - By this I mean someone with a dog in the fight, a dog in the hunt (I like the hunting better than the fighting.), skin in the game, a horse in the race. These people truly cannot see your situation clearly enough to give solid advice because they have some kind of an investment in the outcome.

Here is an example: Over the years I have counseled numerous couples who had physical-abuse issues in the marriage, most often the husband being the abuser. Not being emotionally attached to either spouse, I was able to view the situation impartially and make the appropriate recommendations to end the abuse and re-build the relationship. I can tell you for a fact that if the wife was my own daughter, it would be extremely difficult for me to be an impartial, effective counselor. I am way too close to the situation. My fatherly love for my daughter, my overly protective nature, my disappointment in my son-in-law, and the concern for my grandchildren would all exclude me from being their counselor.

Have you ever heard the saying "You can't see the forest for the trees?" It means that when you are in the forest, the trees directly in front of you block your view of the whole forest. Likewise in your marriage, you are caught up in the details of what is going on and cannot see the big picture. People who are too close to you are in the forest with you, and that will also limit their vision and dramatically taint the quality of their advice.

• **Non-Christians** - The very first verse in the Book of Psalms reads:

> "Blessed is the man who walks not in the counsel of the ungodly, Nor stands in the path of sinners, Nor sits in the seat of the scornful."

If you are a born-again, Bible-believing Christian, non-Christians are not qualified to give you any important marital advice. The reality is, they don't understand where you are coming from because their view of the world is secular, not spiritual. The Holy Spirit does not dwell in non-Christians, so they can only use what they know in the flesh to advise anyone. 1 Corinthians 2:14 describes it this way: "But the natural man does not receive the things of the Spirit of God, for they are foolishness to him; nor can he know them, because they are spiritually discerned."

So let me assume (and you know what they say about assuming) that you agree with only seeking advice from Christians. I need to make an additional point; and that is, you need to be as sure as you possibly can that your advisor is really a Christian. You must be able to see the Christianity in his or her actions, not just hear it in the person's words.

Demonstrated by the continuing re-election of politicians who do not bring their campaign promises to fruition, our culture puts a lot of emphasis on what people say instead of what they actually do. A 2012 Gallup poll found that "the large majority of Americans—77% of the adult population—*identify with* a Christian religion." I'm not sure what the term *identify with* means. Because I was born in the Bronx to a family of die-hard baseball fans, I identify with the New York Yankees, but that doesn't make me their shortstop.

Years ago I spoke to a woman whose husband had an affair but put an end to it and begged for her forgiveness. The advice she received from the "Christian" women in her BIBLE STUDY was unanimous. They told her to divorce him! I think the Bible they were studying may have been the NAC (Not A Clue) translation. In Philippians 3:3, the apostle Paul gives us one of the best biblical descriptions of a Christian. He writes that true Christians are those who

1. Worship God in the Spirit,
2. Glory in Christ, and
3. Put no confidence in the flesh.

Number 3 is very important because it means that the advice that a true Christian gives someone should never be based on what he or she thinks but rather what God thinks.

If you take the time to search for people who meet these qualifications or are striving daily to meet them, you will most probably get the direction that you need. Notice I used the word *need*. Others will be glad to tell you what you want to hear. God and those who are open to be used by Him will tell you what you need to hear. It's up to you to receive it.

• **Social Media** - I never thought in a million, gazillion, larger-than-the-national-debt years that I would ever have to write this, but here it is. Do not—once again, DO NOT—ask for advice on anything involving your marriage from people on social media. The first time someone told me about sharing their marriage issues with people on social media, I almost fell off my rather comfortable chair. I'm not talking about private e-mails; I mean out-in-the-open, for-all-the-world-to-see, totally exposed discussions of your marital problems.

One couple I was seeing made a daily habit of soliciting advice from their social media "friends" on the most personal of issues. In one session the wife admitted to me that she asked for advice on how to improve her husband's inadequate "bedroom performance." She got so many replies, even from people she had never met, that she could not read them all; and one male "friend" asked for her phone number. And just in case you are wondering, it did not escape my finely tuned hearing when she used the word *performance*. I never liked that word used in the context of a couple's sexual intimacy. It evokes in my mind images of standing ovations, curtain calls, rave reviews, or being booed off the stage. But I saved my thoughts for another session.

Wait, I'm not finished. The husband also admitted that he was on social media getting advice on how to deal with his marriage problems from none other than, are you ready? HIS EX-WIFE! Are you kidding me? Seriously, you can't make this stuff up!

People like this couple, who use the social media to expose themselves and air their grievances (aka dirty laundry) in the public forum, obviously don't understand, or don't care, about the consequences of their actions. Do they care about the embarrassment or humiliation suffered by their children or loved ones who may read what is written? Do they understand the difficulty of trying to take back something that they write about their spouse once it is "posted"? Are they expecting counseling expertise from the same people who spend an exorbitant amount of time detailing to the world everything they did that day while introducing us to their latest "selfie?"

Listen, because I use it myself, I get the fact that there are a number of redeeming factors concerning the use of social media. However, if you think that it is the place to go for advice to reconcile your marriage issues, you are truly mistaken.

~ PRAYER ~

Father, thank you for the story of Solomon and how he rejected the materialism of the world in order to gain the wisdom that only you can provide. Thank you for the book of Proverbs, which gives us clear examples of your divine wisdom. Allow me to use that wisdom, which is mine for the asking, in order serve you and your people.

MORE TO LOVE

Proverbs 12:15

Ecclesiastes 4:13

Proverbs 19:20

REFLECTION/DISCUSSION

1. List the criteria you use to choose someone from whom you will take advice.

2. Describe the last time you were given bad advice from someone you trusted.

3. If your close friend was having an affair and you knew about it, explain what your course of action would be.

4. Describe a situation in your life that would benefit from Christian counseling.

LESSON 7

Work at It

"Do you not know that in a race all the runners run, but only one gets the prize? Run in such a way as to get the prize."

1 Corinthians 9:24

The Bible

OK. So you accepted Christ as your Lord and Savior and shortly after that you got baptized (total submersion and gasping for air). That's it. You are done. You can enjoy your Christianity until you leave that decrepit earthly body of yours and rise to spend eternity in glory. Hallelujah! You are now a person of faith.

So one day, as you habitually skim through your Bible, which you think is not really necessary since you have already achieved absolute, undeniable, irrevocable salvation, you just happen to stumble upon (or so you believe) 2 Peter 1:5-8. It reads, "For this very reason, make every effort to add to your faith goodness; and to goodness, knowledge; and to knowledge, self-control; and to self-control, perseverance; and to perseverance, godliness; and to godliness, brotherly kindness; and to brotherly kindness, love. For if you possess these qualities in increasing measure, they will keep you from being ineffective and unproductive in your knowledge of our Lord Jesus Christ."

"Hey, wait a minute," you protest. "What's this 'add to' and 'increasing measure' mean?" You thought you were done. This says you have to keep working and improving. You had a feeling when you entered into this born again thing that there might be fine print, and here it is. This salvation thing was misrepresented. You should have demanded full disclosure!

So if you want full disclosure, here it is. When you decide to give your life over to Christ, your work is not over; on the contrary, it is just beginning. Actually, let me clarify this a little. You certainly can ask Christ into your life and one day receive your eternal heavenly reward. But as the previous verses from 2 Peter describe, God wants us to grow, to be effective, and to be productive. He wants us to mimic His life here on earth, and that takes work and sometimes sacrifice. Jesus said in Luke 9:23, "If anyone desires to come after me, let him deny himself, and take up his cross daily, and follow me."

The apostle Paul certainly knew about the hard work involved in being a true disciple. In 2 Corinthians 11:23-28, he describes the hardships he had to go through to bring the Gospel to the unsaved. He writes:

> "I have worked harder, been put in prison more often, been whipped times without number, and faced death again and again. Five times the Jewish leaders gave me thirty-nine lashes. Three times I was beaten with rods. Once I was stoned. Three times I was shipwrecked. Once I spent a whole night and a day adrift at sea. I have traveled on many long journeys. I have faced dangers from rivers and from robbers. I have faced dangers from my own people, the Jews, as well as from the Gentiles.

I have faced dangers in the cities, in the deserts, and on the seas. And I have faced danger from men who claim to be believers but are not. I have worked hard and long, enduring many sleepless nights. I have been hungry and thirsty and have often gone without food. I have shivered in the cold, without enough clothing to keep me warm. Then besides all this I have the daily burden of my concern for all the churches." (NLT)

Ask yourself this question: If you were Paul and you knew ahead of time the hardships and the work that lay ahead of you, would you still choose to be a disciple?

If you want to see a good example of working at something, think about the constant work it takes for us to keep the Ten Commandments that God Himself gave to Moses. I know that some Christians shy away from the word *commandments* and think it should be replaced with *suggestions, proposals,* or *recommendations.* Using words like that would be more in line with a society like ours that prefers relativism to absolute truth. However, God etched them in stone in order to demonstrate that following them is not optional. It reminds me a little of the rules I would lay down for my daughter when she was a teenager. I would say things like, "Your curfew is midnight, and that is etched in stone!"

I have to admit that early on in my pre-Christian years there were a few of the "Commandments" that I had to constantly work at. My rebellious years as a teenager did not always honor my father and my mother. In early adulthood I had a hard time keeping God the number one priority in my life because my work schedule almost always came ahead of Him. I also struggled with coveting what other people had, like nicer cars, bigger houses, and heftier bank accounts. I even thought that it was perfectly acceptable to lie under certain circumstances, especially if it was "a little white one." In contrast, I always thought that obedience to the "shall not murder" command-ment was easy—that is until I moved to Florida and had to contend with the drivers here! Don't worry, I'm working at it.

Understanding and embracing my imperfect Christianity is such a blessing to me. It gives me a freedom that I did not have for a good part of my life. I strive each day to be a better dis-ciple than I was yesterday, but the pressure to be perfect is no longer with me. God, in His infinite wisdom, sent His perfect Son to bear my sins so that I can be imperfect yet attain an eternal life. Romans 3:23-24 concurs: "For all have sinned and fall short of the glory of God, being justified freely by His grace through the redemption that is in Christ Jesus."

Christians who feel guilty over the fact that they do not lead perfect, sinless lives have missed the purpose of a savior. But that does not mean that God does not expect us to give it our all when we choose to follow Him. Christians who believe they do not need to work at their walk with God do not know the true meaning of discipleship.

The Golf Game

So let's get something straight right away. You are NEVER going to make significant improvements in your golf game if you do not practice. If you understand that, nod your head so I don't have to say it again. Good. Thank you.

After my first five years of playing, I reached a handicap level that did not move more than one or two strokes either way for the next 20 years! During those years I took some lessons, watched instructional videos, and subscribed to golf magazines, but the truth of the matter was I was unwilling to practice. I loved to go out and play, but I refused to seriously practice. So now in retrospect, I look back and ask myself what planet was I residing on that allowed me to believe that I would improve my golf game if I was unwilling to WORK AT IT!

I was finally able to improve my handicap about ten years ago, when I decided that I would actually practice. At that time, I was playing twice a week and decided to eliminate one of those playing days and replace it with a day of practice. For at least two hours, I would practice sand shots, chipping, putting, long irons, short irons, you name it. All the while I was doing this, I would see people going out on the course to play, and I wanted to go with them instead of this stupid practicing. But I was committed to improving my game, and after three months of this regimen my handicap dropped by six strokes. Working at it paid off big time!

One of the reasons I enjoy watching professional golfers play is because I know and appreciate how much hard work they put in to play at that level. What we are seeing on television are the results of years of hard work. If you ever get a chance to read about how often, how long, and how intensely pro golfers practice, you will be amazed. The golf website www. thesandtrap.com describes the typical practice day of a well-known player, and it goes like this:

6:00 a.m.—wake up

6:30-8:00—workout with weights

9:00-11:00—hit balls on practice tee

11:00-11:30—practice putting

11:30-12:30 p.m.—play nine holes

12:30-1:00—lunch

1:00-3:00—hit balls on practice tee
3:00-4:00—short game practice
4:00-5:00—play nine holes
5:00-5:30—hit more balls
5:30-6:00—practice putting

I don't know about you, but I'm exhausted just reading this! Excuse me. I need to take a nap. I'll be back shortly.

I'm back. Now where were we? Ah yes, we were talking about the practice habits of professional golfers. Keep in mind that these guys play golf for a living, so their income depends on how well they play. It is no accident or coincidence that the pros are so good. Arnold Palmer said, "It's a funny thing, the more I practice the luckier I get." Granted, practice habits and time allotment of the pros are something that the average recreational golfers do not have; but they demonstrate that all levels of golfers, from the number one ranked golfer in the world to the once-a-year hacker, have to work in order to improve their game.

On a personal note, my favorite (and only) son-in-law Todd is a very talented golfer. He is married to my favorite (and only) daughter, and they have two young children. His family responsibilities, along with a very demanding work schedule, give him little or no time for practice. This works out extraordinarily well for me because his lack of practice, plus the generous amount of handicap strokes he must give me, allows me to occasionally be competitive with him in our matches. If he ever gets the time to practice, it will be a sad time for me. I will be forced to forgo our golf matches and challenge him to shuffleboard instead.

Unfortunately, no matter how long or hard we practice, none of us will ever reach a point where there is no room for improvement We have all heard at one time or another the old axiom "Practice makes perfect." Well, whoever originally said that surely was not talking about golf, because every pro golfer knows that no matter how hard you work, "perfection" is not possible. Gay Brewer, the 1967 Masters Champion, said, "Golf is a game you can never get too good at. You can improve, but you can never get to where you master the game." The reason I like that quote so much is because it epitomizes the way I approach golf. I always want to be improving, but "mastering" the game for me is out of the question because it is out of my reach. Thinking like that takes the burden of trying to be perfect off my shoulders and allows me to "work at it" at my own pace while I enjoy playing.

The Marriage

For me, the hardest work I have ever done is trying to be a good parent. Notice I said good parent, because being a bad parent is a much easier task. I know this because I have met so many bad parents. The very close second hardest work I have ever done is trying to be a good spouse. I know that because I stumble a lot (and occasionally fall) in my attempt to be one.

When I do pre-marital counseling with a young couple, one of the first things I ask each of them is why they want to get married. Typically, the wife-to-be will get a dreamy look in her eyes, look longingly at her future husband, and say, "I love him more than anything in the world. He is the man I have waited for all my life. He is my knight in shining armor, and

I want to spend the rest of my life with him." The guy will look at me without expression because he's thinking about the playoff game he's missing and mumble, "I love her too." I may be exaggerating a little here, but you get the idea. The point is, EVERY couple that I have ever had in pre-marital counseling told me with different levels of enthusiasm that they loved each other. Furthermore, allow me to go out on a limb here and say that there is probably a minuscule percentage of couples in our culture who were not in love when they got married.

If I am correct, then why are there so many horrible marriages, separations, and divorces? The answer is simple: LOVE IS NOT ENOUGH! Marriage presents many issues that require work. Loving each other certainly helps, but if you are not willing to work at your marriage, love alone will not sustain it. Back in the day, there was a singing duo called Captain and Tennille. They had a hit single in 1975 called "Love Will Keep Us Together." Sorry guys—good song but inaccurate premise. Today I would change the song title to "Love and Working at It Will Keep Us Together." I'm not sure it would be a hit, but at least it would be true.

Most Christian weddings that I have officiated or attended in my life include a reading from Scripture chosen by the couple being married. In theory, the couple should fully understand the meaning of the verse or verses and recognize how these words apply to their new lives as husband and wife. One of the most often used Scripture verses is 1 Corinthians 13:4-7, often called the "Love Verses" because they describe so eloquently the various attributes of biblical love. Let's read starting at verse 4:

> "Love is patient and kind. Love is not jealous or boastful or proud or rude. It does not demand its own way. It is

not irritable, and it keeps no record of being wronged. It does not rejoice about injustice but rejoices whenever the truth wins out. Love never gives up, never loses faith, is always hopeful, and endures every circumstance." (NLT)

Wow! Now that's the description of love that romance novels are made of! It's romantic, blissful, passionate, tender, and even euphoric. But at the risk of sounding like a pessimistic old married man, that description of biblical love sounds to me like a LOT OF WORK! And it sounds like a lot of work because the behavior described does not come naturally to me or to most people, especially those I come in contact with in my marriage counseling sessions. I look at the attributes of love in these verses and realize how much time and effort it would take for a couple to achieve this type of love. It is imperative that couples understand that the love described in these verses is not based on emotion; it is based on action. In other words, this type of love needs to be visible and experienced. Saying "I love you" is not enough. You need to prove your love through your actions.

Husbands - Are you "patient" with your wife as she relates every detail of a story that you think she is taking far too long to tell? Do you go out of your way to show your wife "kindness" even when you don't feel like it? Do you often "demand" that things be done your way?

Wives - Do you find yourself "irritable" at your husband's refusal to place dirty laundry where it belongs or his inability to understand what "put the seat down" means? Do you remember things he has done "wrong" in the past and bring them up when you feel the need? Have you ever thought or said "I give up" in anger over your husband's behavior?

In all fairness, the odds are stacked against any of us achieving this type of love fully because it is how Jesus loves us. Try substituting His name everywhere you see the word "love" in the verses and you will see the truth in 1 John 4:8 that declares "God is love." I am not bringing this up to discourage you but to point out that you have your work cut out for you. I firmly believe that if every married couple was determined, with His help, to follow the example of Christ for loving each other, they would be shocked at the positive results.

There are occasions when I will do what is known as intensive counseling with couples who are on the verge of divorce and are willing to give it one more try. Counseling sessions occur over a three-to-five-consecutive-day period, with each session lasting approximately four hours. Couples that want to do this are in for an enormous amount of work to get them to a point where God can reconcile their marriage; and the process inevitably leaves everyone, including me, mentally and emotionally exhausted. Therefore, before I agree to this form of counseling, I carefully question each one of them to determine how hard they each are willing to work to salvage the marriage. I explain that if BOTH of them agree to do everything I ask of them and put out a 100% effort, then there is a very good chance that they, with God's direction, can get their marriage back on track. If they are not willing, it will all be a waste of time.

It saddens me to see how many couples decide to skip the counseling and proceed directly to divorce. One couple actually told me the following: "We still love each other; but after all these years of fighting, we don't want to work at this marriage anymore and would rather divorce and start over with someone new."

Their attitude reminded me of our behavior as consumers. We have always liked disposable products that required less attention and work, like diapers, contact lenses, shaving razors, and plastic "silverware." So it probably makes some sort of weird sense that our view of marriage would follow suit. When having a successful marriage gets to be too much work, simply dispose of it and get a new one! The disposable marriage philosophy may be acceptable in our culture, but it runs contrary to God's Word that promotes a lifelong commitment.

~ PRAYER ~

Father, teach me to be a true disciple of your Son, not just in my words but each and every day in my actions. I want to be a tireless servant of yours who will follow your lead in all I do. Help me to grow in my faith and deeds to more profoundly exhibit to the world my love for you. When I grow weary, give me the strength and perseverance to continue the work that you set before me.

MORE TO LOVE

Colossians 3:23

Ecclesiastes 7:20

Proverbs 14:23

REFLECTION/DISCUSSION

1. What are the ongoing issues in your marriage that you and your spouse have worked at with little or no success?

2. Are there any marital issues you have that you would describe as "hopeless?" What makes them "hopeless?"

3. Name something that you have always been mediocre at that you would like to be really good at.

4. Give an example of a relationship other than marriage that requires you to work hard at maintaining or improving.

LESSON 8

Pray

"Pray without ceasing."

1 Thessalonians 5:17

The Bible

There are many Bible verses and stories concerning the power of prayer. One of my favorites is Philippians 4:6-7 because it deals with the common condition of anxiety. It reminds us to "be anxious for nothing, but in everything by prayer and supplication, with thanksgiving, let your requests be known to God; and the peace of God which surpasses all understanding, will guard your hearts and minds through Christ Jesus." This means that when you are anxious or worried about ANYTHING, you can pray earnestly and thankfully and receive the true peace that only God can bring.

I have a friend, Nancy Peters, who taught me in my early Christian years the meaning of the word *everything* in that verse. The first church that we attended had a short time during the service for the congregation to make prayer requests. Nancy would often stand up and ask the congregation to pray for any and all the things in her life that were causing her or her family to be troubled. She sought prayer for lost keys, improved school grades for her children, dead car batteries, and other non-life-threatening issues. My fledgling faith caused me to wonder why this woman would bother the Almighty with, in my mind, such trivial requests. I figured God was dealing with the big stuff like widespread hunger, outbreaks of disease, and the never-ending conflicts around the world; and she wanted to pull Him away from those things to help her find her keys! What was she thinking? She was apparently thinking that the God who created the entire universe, placed every star exactly where He wanted, and named them all was able to multi-task. I am so thankful that I now think as she does. If I didn't, I wouldn't be able to write this book because He's always answering my prayers for finding my misplaced eyeglasses.

God makes it very clear that although He is God, He is always totally accessible to us. The writer of Hebrews encourages us in 4:16 by writing: "Let us therefore come boldly to the throne of grace, that we may obtain mercy and find grace to help us in our time of need." I love the fact that the God that I worship allows me to come straight to Him for everything. I often use that verse to explain to people how much God wants us to develop a personal and intimate relationship with Him. I can't think of one leader of any nation in the world today whose door is open to anyone who would like to speak to him or her. Yet the King over all the universe not only welcomes but encourages everyone to speak to Him directly anytime we wish.

Like most, but not all, Christians I got a real breakthrough in my prayer life when I realized that God did not expect my prayers to be formal or eloquent. That was really fine with me because I have never been described as formal or eloquent. I remember the first time I heard someone pray aloud in church and it caused me to be very impressed and discouraged at the same time. The prayer lasted at least two hours. (Well, maybe I'm exaggerating, but it was at least two or three minutes.) It was filled with verbatim Scripture verses from the King James Version and was so beautifully flowing and poetic that I sat there with my mouth open in awe. My joy at what I had just heard quickly gave way to a sinking feeling of discouragement; if that was the way to talk to God, I was in deep trouble because I don't speak like that.

Needless to say, I was relieved to read what Jesus had to say about prayer in Matthew 6:7-8: "And when you pray, do not use vain repetitions as the heathen do. For they think that they will be heard for their many words. Therefore do not be like them. For your Father knows the things you have need of before you ask Him." What good news! God doesn't need a lot of words because He already knows what you want. As a matter of fact, it was Martin Luther who said, "The fewer the words the better the prayer."

I don't want to be misunderstood. I'm not here to tell anyone what a sincere, heartfelt prayer should sound like or how long it should be. I'm simply saying that short, sweet, and to the point is fine with God and works well for me and my previously mentioned eyeglasses.

As we study prayer in the Bible, there are several important lessons that will help us develop a more effective prayer life:

• **Pray for the right reasons.** James 4:3 gives us some insight into this concept: "You ask and do not receive, because you ask amiss, that you may spend it on your own pleasures." Simply stated, you must always check your motives when you ask God for anything.

Let's re-visit the discussion between Solomon and God in 1 Kings 3:9 and listen to Solomon tell God what his motives are for wanting wisdom. "Therefore give to your servant an understanding heart to judge your people, that I may discern between good and evil. For who is able to judge this great people of yours?" Solomon asked for wisdom so that he could better serve God. In making his request, he not only took God's will into consideration, he made it his priority.

Even churches need to check the motivation of their prayers. A common prayer in most churches is that they grow in the number of people who attend. If their growth prayers are for bringing people to Christ, creating disciples who will in turn create more disciples, and having more people and money to reach out into the community as witnesses to God's love, they are praying for the right reason.

• **Pray with legs.** That means while you are praying you should also be moving in the direction of your prayer.

"Alex," who had not had a steady job for a number of years, was asking our church for help paying his bills once again. The church had a benevolent fund and was happy to help people in times of need. As usual, I asked him if he had gotten a job yet and he answered in the same way he always did: "No, but the Lord will provide." One time I felt led to ask him how many job applications he had filled out or interviews he had gone to since I last saw him several months ago. His answer was "None, but I continue to pray that the Lord will provide." That is a great example of NOT praying with legs.

There are times when we all need to be still and wait on God, but the Bible shows us in numerous places how God likes to multiply our efforts rather than just hand things to us. In

Matthew 14, Jesus feeds five thousand people by multiplying the five loaves and the two fish that he made His disciples bring to Him. Peter had to go catch a fish and pull the coin out of its mouth to pay the taxes. Proverbs 14:23 points out: "All hard work brings a profit, but mere talk leads only to poverty."

Like all of us, "Alex" needs to pray for his financial provision, but the answer to his prayer may be in the job that God has waiting for him if he ever decides to apply for it.

In the Old Testament, Nehemiah was rebuilding the destroyed walls around Jerusalem. He knew that his enemies were conspiring to attack before the protective wall was finished, so in the ninth verse of chapter four, Nehemiah writes, "Nevertheless, we made our prayer to our God, and because of them we set a watch against them day and night." Nehemiah was "praying with legs."

The Bible points out in Psalm 103:3 that it is God who heals all our diseases, and I believe that to be unequivocally true. I always seek His healing for any ailment that afflicts me. Does that mean that I should never seek the advice of a doctor or take an appropriate medication? No, because God can, and does, use the people and the medications that HE created to accomplish His work. Therefore, I depend upon God for my healing, but I employ the wisdom that He gave me to decide what medical care I may need. Keep praying, but keep moving!

• **Pray with faith.** If you don't expect God to answer your prayer, it doesn't make much sense to pray in the first place, does it? In Acts 12, members of the early church were gathered at the house of Mary, the mother of John, praying for Peter, who was in jail. While they were praying, an angel of the Lord came to the jail and miraculously released Peter, who went directly to Mary's house to share the good news. However, when a girl named Rhoda responded to his knocking at the door, she didn't let him in but instead ran back to the group to announce Peter's arrival. Well, lo and behold, nobody believed her. When she finally convinced them that she wasn't crazy, they went to the door and were "astonished" when they saw Peter. So here were people in the early church praying for Peter to be released; and when God answered their prayer, they didn't believe it!

I wish I could truthfully say that Christians in today's churches are different. One woman recently told me that she has been praying for her husband's salvation for many years but she doesn't believe he will ever submit himself to Christ. I suggested that she re-read James 1 in order to understand the error she was making. Verses 6-8 describe how we should ask God for anything:

> "But let him ask in faith, with no doubting, for he who doubts is like a wave of the sea driven and tossed by the wind. For let not that man suppose that he will receive anything from the Lord: he is a double-minded man, unstable in all his ways."

There is a plaque in my daughter's house that reads, "Faith is not knowing that God can answer your prayers, it is knowing that He will answer your prayers."

• **Accept His timing.** If you often find yourself being impatient with God's timing, welcome to the club. Don't get excited. It's not an exclusive club; anyone can join. As a matter of fact, I'm a longtime member. I know that God hears my prayers. I also know that God will eventually answer my prayers. I just can't wrap my head around the idea of waiting. The danger of not waiting on God is the possibility of jumping ahead of Him and settling for something less than He would have produced had I waited.

I remember a day 30 years ago when my then five-year-old daughter, Larissa, was asking me to buy her a late-afternoon ice-cream cone. Knowing that it would spoil her appetite for dinner, I told her she could have one later, after her meal. Like any child her age, her lack of patience and need for immediate gratification caused her to argue the point. I responded by offering this proposal: "If you wait until after dinner, I will buy you an ice-cream cone tonight and every night for the next two weeks. But if you insist on having it now, you can have it, but you will get no ice cream at all for the next two weeks. The choice was simple for her: "Give it to me now!" She was not very happy over the following two weeks, but I believe she was taught a valuable, biblically based lesson.

Be aware that while we may think we are waiting on God, the truth may be that He is waiting on us. One of the questions we need to ask ourselves during any waiting period is whether or not we are ready for God to answer our prayers.

Because they could not be obedient to God's commands and stop their grumbling, God rightly determined that the Israelites were not ready to enter the Promised Land until they had wandered in the desert for 40 years.

In 1 Samuel 16, God instructs Samuel to anoint the teen-aged David king, but it was a number of years and some very harsh trials that David had to go through before he actually took the throne. It was during this waiting period that David was able to learn perseverance, humility, and total dependence on God for his provision. Some of his beautiful prayers for salvation from his enemies in the Book of Psalms give us a good idea of his commitment to being patient. In Psalm 27:14 David encourages us to "wait for the Lord; be strong and take heart and wait for the Lord."

Waiting on God to answer our prayers may be difficult, but understanding how perfect His timing really is makes it a lot easier.

The Golf Game

I know exactly what you are thinking. Of course you need to pray on the golf course. You need to pray for straighter drives, more accurate putts, better scores, not making a fool of yourself in front of your friends, and, in my case, beating my son-in-law. The problem I see with these prayers is that I really don't understand how the granting of these requests brings glory to God. For a Christian, the golf course should be a place where you cannot only have a great time but also a place where you can continue and even enhance your prayer life.

I actually remember the first time I ever prayed while playing golf. I was in a three-day tournament in upstate New York with a large group of men that I played with on Long Island. I was a very new Christian, and I wasn't really sure if God would appreciate me praying for anything on a golf course. The first day, I massacred a par three hole so badly that I wound up taking a nine while my three playing partners watched in amazement and wondered how anyone could be so inept. The ironic part was the fact that the hole had a gigantic green that was pretty easy to land on, but if you missed it you were in BIG trouble like me. The next day, I had to play the same hole, and as I stood on the tee box I silently prayed (today I would make it quite audible), "Lord, please let my ball land on the green." I struck the ball very well and watched as it landed on the green and rolled towards the hole, literally stopping one inch from it. One more inch would have been a hole in one that would have awarded me a ONE THOUSAND DOLLAR tournament prize. Unfortunately, my first reaction was not gratefulness for my answered prayer but regret for not praying for a hole in one!

That incident taught me two valuable lessons concerning golfing and praying. The first lesson was that you can indeed pray that you play well, as long as God gets the credit. After winning the 2007 Masters, Zach Johnson proclaimed, "Being Easter, my goal was to glorify God, and hopefully I did that today." The second lesson was to pray more boldly. For instance, my prayer should have been, "Lord, yesterday I totaled a nine on this miserable par three. Today I want you to give me a hole-in-one. Amen. P.S. I will give you all the credit and tithe my winnings."

Because golf can sometimes be a very frustrating game (you think?), I always pray before I play that I will be a good witness to those I am playing with. Believe me, when you are not playing well, that is not easy to do. Philippians 4:13 tells me, "I can do all things through Christ who strengthens me," and I have used that verse many times to keep my composure after missing an easy putt. One of my all-time favorite pro golfers, Chi Chi Rodriguez, said, "I never pray to God to make a putt. I pray to God to help me react good if I miss a putt."

Many of the golfers I play with like to tease me about having an unfair advantage in matches because I am a pastor and God will help me win. Whenever I sink a long putt or hit a really good shot, they accuse me of successfully praying for that outcome. When this happens, I simply remind them that I always play by the rules and repeat a quote from the renowned British golf writer Henry Longhurst. He warned, "If you call on God to improve the results of a shot while it is still in motion, you are using an 'outside agency' and subject to appropriate penalties under the rules of golf." That usually ends the conversation.

The PGA Tour has no shortage of praying golfers. Pros like Bubba Watson, Ben Crane, Hunter Mahan, Zach Johnson, and dozens of others attend a Bible study and prayer meeting held Wednesday evenings during tournament weeks. After winning the 2012 U.S. Open by one stroke, Web Simpson confessed to NBC commentator Bob Costas, "I probably prayed more on the last three holes than I ever did in my life."

I like to pray before I do just about anything, and golf is no exception. Over the years, I have developed a short prayer before each golf round that includes the following:

- **Thankfulness** - I am humbled by the fact that I have the health, the finances, and the time to have fun, exercise, and fellowship when others do not. I am truly thankful for that.

- **Witnessing** - I want to be a great witness to who God is and what He has done in my life. My language, temperament, and attitude need to glorify God and not the world.

- **Encouragement** - Romans 12:8 identifies encouragement as a spiritual gift. In recent years, God has showered me with opportunities to use this gift to minister to others in all areas of my life. The golf course can be a discouraging place for some; and if God directs me to give them words of encouragement, I will jump at the chance.

- **Intercession** - I consider myself very fortunate because of all the opportunities I have to pray for people on the golf course. Without prying into people's business, I will always try to discern if there is a specific issue that someone needs prayer for; and I try my best to let them know that it would be both a blessing and a privilege for me to intercede on their behalf before God.

The Marriage

Too many Christian couples treat God as just another guest who was invited to the wedding ceremony and the reception but had to go back from where He came from afterwards. If you included God in your wedding, He should be included in all aspects of your marriage. With God, it's all or nothing. He does not want the lukewarm Christian, and He asks us in Matthew 12:30 to make the choice of being for or against Him, with no neutral ground. He wants to talk with you each morning when you awake and help you both plan your day. He wants to be part of your daily routine and give you advice and answer your questions. He wants to be at the dinner table with you each night and have wonderful fellowship talking about how your day went. And He wants to be with you as you thank Him for His blessings and lay your head down for a peaceful sleep.

In marriage, praying together usually means staying together. There is no doubt that the couples I know who have a strong, consistent prayer life are able to more successfully resolve the issues they face in their marriage. Jesus said in Matthew 18:19-20, "Again I say to you that if two of you agree on earth concerning anything that you ask, it will be done for them by my Father in heaven. For where two or three are gathered together in my name, I am there in the midst of them." That is why one of the first questions I ask of couples in need of counseling is "Do you pray together as a couple?" Guess what the most popular answer to that question is. (Hint: They're in counseling!)

In my own counseling experience I have observed numerous benefits of couples praying together, and these are a few of what I feel are the most important:

• **Praying together as a couple creates intimate communication.** The term *intimacy* in the marriage setting is too often associated with having sex. When I first ask couples to describe the intimacy in their marriage, the majority immediately begin to describe issues regarding the actual sex act. Although sex is obviously an important part of marriage, it is only a small segment of true intimacy. That is the reason why so many couples in crisis do not have problems in the bedroom, but their lack of emotional and intellectual intimacy is destroying their marriage.

Emotional intimacy comes when couples are able to safely share their fears, anxieties, regrets, sadness, hopes, dreams, and joys. A deep bond will develop as couples share these thoughts and pray for each other. I must note that sharing what your spouse tells you during these conversations with people outside your marriage, like family or friends, can and probably will have negative effects on your relationship. Doing so is a serious form of betrayal, so don't even think about it.

Intellectual intimacy happens when couples simply talk to each other about the things they enjoy or subjects that interest them. My wife, Debbie, has always been interested in the health and wellness industry. She has introduced me to water aerobics, aroma therapy, homeopathic medicine, and a host of other areas that I probably never would have looked at on my own. My interest in politics has caused us to have many lively, thought-provoking conversations. We love talking about house design, travel, and great restaurants. Showing your spouse that you enjoy having conversations with him or her on all types of subjects will go a long way in developing closeness in your relationship.

• **Praying together as a couple promotes balance.** "Pete" and "Lisa" told me an all-too-familiar story. After 30 plus years of marriage, their three kids were out of the house, married, and living in other states. These parents had devoted themselves totally to their children; and subjects like school, sports, and summer camp were the topics of all the conversations they had as a couple. Now that the children were gone, they both felt that there was nothing to talk about because they really didn't know each other. Unfortunately, they were right. They had spent too much time being parents and not enough time being a couple. When couples have children, it is imperative that they pray for balance in their lives. Your roles as a parent and a spouse deserve equal attention, so couples should always be praying for balance in the various roles that they play.

• **Praying together as a couple displays humility**. Few things bring couples closer than the knowledge that they cannot solve the difficult issues that confront them without God's help. When those major problems hit your relationship (notice I said when and not if), going to God in prayer should be your first line of defense. When couples humble themselves before God, a sense of peace will come over them because their burdens have been shifted over to His very broad shoulders.

• **Praying together as a couple is a great witness.** Yes, it is a great witness to other people when they know that the two of you pray together; but more importantly, what does it teach your children? For those of you who don't already know this, let me make this perfectly clear. (There will be a bonus for anyone who knows which U.S. President made the statement "Let me make this perfectly clear" famous.) I apologize for the digression. Anyway, my point is that your children will always learn from what they see you do, not from what you say. As they watch the two of you pray together, or better yet lead the family in prayer, your children will be more likely to marry someone with that same mindset.

~ PRAYER ~

Father, thank you for revealing to us the awesome power of prayer. Thank you for allowing us to approach your throne of grace with boldness to receive your mercy and grace. I thank you for all the prayers you have answered in my life, and I humbly thank you in advance for all my answered prayers that have yet to come.

MORE TO LOVE

Mark 11:24

Colossians 4:2

Romans 12:12

REFLECTION/DISCUSSION

1. When faced with a serious problem or decision in your life, is prayer your "first line of defense" or your "last-ditch effort?"

2. Give specific examples of things that you pray for during the normal day.

3. Do you and your spouse set aside time each day specifically for praying together? Why or why not?

4. What is one thing that you have been a long time praying for that God has not given to you? Do you find yourself growing impatient with God's timing?

ABOUT THE AUTHOR

Sal LoPriore is currently the Counseling Pastor at the rapidly growing New Day Christian Church in Port Charlotte, Florida. A native New Yorker, "Pastor Sal" is a Board Certified Pastoral Counselor, Life Coach, and Christian Speaker. He is an active member of the American Association of Christian Counselors and is part of their extensive Christian Care Network. He is also trained and certified in mediation, conflict resolution, and negotiation. Sal completed training in Pastoral Crisis Intervention at the Billy Graham Training Center in Asheville, NC, and is a member of their Rapid Response Team.

Sal has a proven track record as a highly effective Christian Speaker. In recent years he has been the guest speaker at churches and Christian organizations in a number of states, including New York, New Jersey, Georgia, and Florida. The blend of his unique sense of humor and sound scriptural teaching allows his audience to understand even difficult biblical concepts and helps them to incorporate the truth of God's Word into their daily lives.

In 2007 Sal and his wife, Debbie, founded Grand Vista Ministries, Inc. Their "Essentials Project" supplies free toiletries to the hundreds of homeless and needy families throughout Charlotte County, Florida.

During the summer months, Sal and Debbie can be found at their retreat in the mountains of North Georgia. It is there that Sal does three-, four-, or five-day Intensive Marriage Counseling with couples on the verge of divorce while also maintaining an e-counseling schedule with his Florida clients.

In his free time Sal can be found reading, walking, biking, and, as you may have guessed, golfing.

For more information or to contact Sal, you can visit his website at www.PastorSal.com.

GLOSSARY OF GOLF TERMS

birdie - A score of 1 under par on a hole (i.e., a score of 4 on a par 5 hole).

bogey - A score of 1 over par for a hole (i.e., a score of 4 on a par 3 hole).

chip - A short approach shot with a low trajectory usually used around the green. Can also be found on the shoulder of some golfers after losing a match.

drive - This term describes your tee shot or your first hit on each hole.

driver - The club that is designed to hit the ball the furthest. Usually only used for a tee shot.

flagstick - A flagstick is a pole with a flag attached that is placed in the hole on each green in order to see the location of the hole from a distance.

hacker - A golfer who is new to the game or not very skilled. Nickname for most golfers at one time or another.

handicap - The number of strokes a player may deduct from his actual (gross) score to adjust his score to that of a scratch golfer, thus leveling the playing field.

handicap system - Keeping in mind that the lower the score in golf the better, this system is designed to allow golfers to compete with golfers better than they are. (i.e., A golfer with a 10 handicap who shoots a 92 for 18 holes has his score adjusted by his handicap, thus making his score 82.)

hole - A 4-inch round receptacle on each green that you try (and try again) to put your ball into.

lie - Where the ball is resting after each shot. What you may be tempted to do to your wife when she asks you if you went to work or played golf.

out-of-bounds - The area outside of the golf course limits in which play is prohibited. If you hit a ball out-of-bounds, you must hit it again from the same spot and take a one-stroke penalty. Also a place where many golf balls with the initials SL written on them can be found.

par - The officially recommended number of strokes that you should take in order to complete a given hole (i.e., a score of 4 on a par 4 hole).

penalty stroke - An additional stroke that is added to a golfer's score for a lost ball or any type of rules violation. Using her trusty wooden spoon, what my Italian grandmother used to give me as a child for misbehaving.

rough - Longer grass areas adjacent to the fairway. Normally you try to avoid the rough. Where I often go to after my tee shot.

scratch golfer - A player who has a handicap of 0. This player will theoretically shoot par on all holes.

stinky - Acceptable word used by unnamed pastor to describe some of his golf shots.

stroke - A swing of a club or putter with the intent of hitting the ball. What I almost had when I got my first hole-in-one!

tee - Term for the area where play begins on a particular hole. (i.e., The fifth tee is where you hit your first shot on the fifth hole.) Type of shirt that is unacceptable attire at most golf clubs.